A Decade in My Life
1969 - 1979
Poems, Photos and a Play

A Decade in My Life
1969 –1979
Poems, Photos and a Play

Etan Boritzer

Poems, Photos, and a Play
1969-1979

© Copyright 2024
First edition 2024

All rights reserved. No part of this publication may be reproduced, stored in a retrieval system, or transmitted in any form or by any means, electronic, mechanical, photocopying, recording, or otherwise without the written permission of the Publisher.

ISBN 979-8-3302-6854-2

Veronica Lane Books
www.VeronicaLaneBooks.com
Books That Make a Difference!

11420 US-1, Suite 124, N. Palm Beach, FL 33408 USA
Tel: +1(833) VLBOOKS (+1 833-852-6657

Dedication

To my dear Mom and Dad, Aunt Gretel, my sister and brother-in-law, gurus and teachers, benefactors and supporters, friends and people I have met for a few moments on the path. My prayers, love, and gratitude are always with you wonderful souls. And yes, thankfully God too has always been with me every step of the way!

Table of Contents

Introduction..1-6

Photo Spread 1...7-8

Photo Spread 2...9-10

Photo Spread 3...11-12

Noon Moon Days..13-34

Photo Spread 4...35-36

Fish Head Soup..37-62

Photo Spread 5...63-64

Photo Spread 6...65-66

Photo Spread 7...67-68

A Sampler..69-82

Photo Spread 8...83-84

Photo Spread 9...85-86

Photo Spread 10...87-88

Diogenes the Cynic...89-114

Photo Spread 11...115-116

Photo Spread 12...117-118

100 Plays..119-221

Photo Spread 13...222-223

Photo Spread 14...224-225

Let Me Explain...

I put everything I like into my paintings. The worse for them, they have to learn to get along with each other.
- Pablo Picasso

I was 12 years old in 1962 and browsing through the 33 RPM album racks in the records dept in the basement of Alexander's Dept. store on Fordham Road in the Bronx when I came upon Bob Dylan's first album. He was staring straight out at me from under his Dutch boy cap and wearing his cool fleece-lined suede jacket. I had no idea who this dude was, but I knew that I had to buy the album, which I did. His poetry knocked out most of us kids.

> *My eyes collide head-on with stuffed*
> *Graveyards, false goals, I scoff*
> *At pettiness which plays so rough*
> *Walk upside down inside handcuffs*
> *Kick my legs to crash it off*
> *Say, okay, I've had enough*
> *What else can you show me?*

Actually, that's from *It's Alright, Ma (I'm Only Bleeding)* Dylan's 5th album *Bringing It All Back Home* released in 1965.

I mean, I was always rebellious and defiant as my black-and-white toddler photos show. My mother told me that in Tel Aviv when the other kids saw me come into the playground, they immediately ran away. *WTF?*

Of course, The Beatles' words influenced us too.

> *I told you about Strawberry Fields*
> *You know the place where nothing is real*
> *Well, here's another place you can go*
> *Where everything flows.*

That's *Glass Onion* from the Beatles' *White Album* released in 1968.

Other early literary influences: Henry Miller, Blaise Cendrars (*"Shit, I yelled from my mother's womb/I don't want to live!"*), Albert Camus, Chuang Tzu, e.e. cummings, and others. Thanks to my mother, who had shelves and shelves of books at home, I always had a book in my hand wherever I traveled or stayed.

I barely made it out of high school but somehow I was able to fake a B average and graduate in 1968. If it were up to me, I would have skipped my senior year at McBurney School for Boys, a small and expensive all-boys prep school on W. 63rd and Central Park West in Manhattan. I would have quit immediately if I could have figured out how to get a job on a merchant ship, my dream career. However, I admit that I did pick up valuable English language and writing skills at McBurney, especially from our English teacher, Mr. Schumann. I still recall that he even taught us how to remember the correct spelling of the word *separate*: there is a rat in *separate*.

I got to McBurney, in the 10th grade because of some altercations with the PRs (Puerto Ricans) at Taft High School in the Bronx. My mother freaked out when she returned one afternoon from her OT job (Occupational Therapist) at Kingsbridge Jewish Home and Hospital for the Aged and she saw the bleeding gash over my left eye. The knife had nicked me there, but I survived with 2 stitches.

Wade Junior High School, which I also attended in the Bronx, became famous after it was discovered that Lee Harvey Oswald had been a student there for a year. Interestingly enough, after the assassination, a few of the wooden desktops in our classrooms had etched in them: *Lee Harvey Oswald Sat Here*. The Bronx is definitely where I got my sick sense of humor. Oh, and BTW, Wade was also important for me because I was first professionally published due to an essay I wrote there on the assassination. Mrs. Rubin, our English teacher, submitted my essay for a tribute anthology to Kennedy by NYC public school kids. I even got to meet RFK at the tribute ceremony!

Unfortunately for my immigrant parents, George and Lotte, I was destined to torture them in my boyhood pubescent days, ages 14 to 18. They finally got rid of me after I somehow graduated from McBurney and embarked on my illustrious college education at Beloit College, in Beloit WI. I started smoking pot when I was 14 and then, hanging out with my other idiot friends on Mt. Eden Ave in the Bronx, I also managed to ingest many varieties of prescription pills, LSD, and other healthy intoxicants such as glue and prescription Robitussin AC (with codeine) which we copped by the caseload from a *farmacia* in Spanish Harlem on 111th Street. Seriously, one time, my friends told me they managed to pull me back in from an open window of some high-rise hotel room we had rented in Manhattan just as I was to accidentally plunge to my death far below. I didn't remember shit about that. My poor parents had to deal with McBurney wanting to kick me out, as well as several serious encounters with the police due to my cheerful drug use. Thankfully, in later years, I made it up to my loving parents who somehow never gave up on me. *Thank you forever, Aba and Ima!*

Speaking of the Bronx and poetry, do you know one of the shortest poems ever written? It was by Ogen Nash.
The Bronx?
No thonx!

Well, Beloit College lasted one 6-month semester and I left there with a D average in early 1969. I was a horny young lad and very busy in that dept while at Beloit. I smoked pot and listened stoned to my jazz albums and didn't attend class much. By that time, I had already *turned on* and *tuned in*, and finally, I could *drop out!* (per Dr. Timothy Leary). I really had no interest in being in the middle of nowhere with another bunch of white middle-class kids, studying for what? I already knew I wanted to be a writer and an actor. I had a role in every school play from elementary school to McBurney, and I loved performing in front of other people. And I am still a ham. In fact, the only difference between Etan and a ham is that a ham can be cured! *Badaboom!*

As to my early writings, our second-grade teacher at P.S. 70 Elementary (Mrs. Cooperman) liked my poems and tacked them on the class bulletin board. At Beloit, I remember our English professor on the first day of class asking, "How many of you here want to be writers?" A few of us raised our hands and he said, "Well, what the hell are you doing here? Why don't you go and write?"

Another thing, I knew even before I got to Beloit, was that I needed badly to go to San Francisco and wear some flowers in my hair and walk around the streets of Haight Ashbury bare-footed. It was the Summer of Love! I was definitely not going back to NYC. My sister Yael and her husband Shlomo were at UC Berkeley earning their doctorates and so of course they welcomed me into their tiny student apartment there—*not!*

Finally, I could go crazy! I found some cooking jobs in Berkeley (I started my cooking career in 1964, age 14, at a sleepover camp in Vermont in exchange for hanging out in the country, far away from the ugly NYC summers). I rented a little room in a big Victorian on McKinley Ave, shared a bathroom and shower with 6 UC students also living there. My room was big and quiet and faced a nice green backyard. And then I did really chase around all those bra-less hippie chicks reeking of patchouli oil, plus get some theatre gigs, and write! I did have one big problem though. I lost my student draft deferment when I quit Beloit. That meant that I was eligible to be drafted and go to Vietnam. I knew that I did not want to go to Vietnam and kill those nice people in their own country. Oh, and possibly die there for no good reason.

Yes, I got nervous about that prospect, and so I did what any rational 18-year-old would do during those times—I became a long-haired, bearded, radicalized Berkeley crazy. We protested the war on campus and in the streets, broke windows at B of A, got chased and arrested by the police. Eventually, Governor Reagan sent in the National Guard during the People's Park riots, pledging to end the disorder, "even if it takes a bloodbath!" Yup, we all clearly remember his words. I was arrested with the other protestors, and thereafter, I actually helped the Black Panthers raise money because the revolution was Now! So, I was already woke back then, OK? Not to mention my horde of multicultural babes.

All this time I was writing poetry and plays and stories on my beat-up old manual typewriter while sitting cross-legged on my floor mattress in my little room—very beat poet/writer was I now! I owned my first restaurant in Berkeley, The Swallow Café, actually co-owned with several others in our socialist/capitalist collective enterprise. These were the heydays of American *nouvelle cuisine* with Alice Waters and Wolfgang Puck in Berkeley and Jeremiah Towers in San Francisco. So, I did improve my culinary game quite a bit during those times.

Also, during this time, I published my first booklet of poems *Noon Moon Days,* included in this tome. I figured if Walt Whitman, Mark Twain, Allen Ginsberg and other great American writers could self-publish, I could too. I sold my poems on campus and then I started hitching to SF and sold them on Fisherman's Wharf ("*Hey, real San Francisco beat poetry right here!* "). I sold the booklet for a dollar but see, my room rent was only $35 a month. That's what an expensive, exclusive prep school education in Manhattan could do for your kid in those days.

I was a very energetic young lad! I was getting acting roles in various SF theatres, doing improv, also doing street mime with a fun, mad little troupe. I published my second booklet of poems *Fish Head Soup*, also included here. In August of 1969, just 8 months after I quit college, I hitched across the country to meet up with my friends Mike and Shelley in NYC to go to a big concert coming up called Woodstock. Yup, I was actually there in that muddy, raining, insane, huge historic music event. I know I was at Woodstock for the full 3 days because I don't remember very much. Mike and Shelley had to remind me that they pulled me away from some Hell's Angels with who I was having a heated argument. Along the way to Woodstock, I stopped back at my alma mater Beloit, and staged a weird mime theatre piece on the campus commons using all my old friends as junior mimes. Then, back to Berkeley with the plane fare help of my dear aunt and mother's sister, Gretel.

Finally, my maritime dream manifested! One of my Berkeley harem's dads, an Israeli, owned a few merchant ships and I was able to connect with him. I sailed as the second cook on the M/V Tropwave, a general cargo carrier, from Cleveland, through the Great Lakes, up the St. Lawrence River (before it froze for the winter) and into the North Atlantic heading for Piraeus, Greece and Israel, with various port stops in between. I learned a lot about institutional cooking from my crazy Yugoslav chief cook, as well as some choice curse words and phrases in Serbian. The sea voyage inspired poems and was exhilarating but I had to work 12 hours a day in the galley cooking 3 meals a day for the 35 crewmembers, 6 days a week plus 'Sunday-at-Sea' for which I was paid double my 55¢ regular hourly wage. Hard work but I loved it! A number of poems from that sea voyage are included in the larger collection here.

I disembarked at the Port of Ashdod, Israel after 6 weeks on board the Tropwave. It was the first time I had been back to Israel since we emigrated when I was 5 years old. I was very excited and nervous too. Immediately, at the passport control, I had a problem. My US passport says, Birthplace: Israel. The passport guy asks me where is my deferment? What deferment? I have the FBI looking for me as a draft dodger in the U.S. but how did they know about me being in Israel? No, my Israeli army deferment. *Whaaa?* Yes, you are military age and an Israeli citizen because you were born here. You need to serve in the army. *Fuck!* I mean, I believe in the Zionist dream and all that but I am just a pot-smoking hippie war protestor from Berkeley, CA! I am not joining anybody's army, dude! Even if you say an Israeli-born person is always an Israeli citizen.

After a few weeks, through bureaucratic hassles and some connected "help," I was finally able to get my Israeli army deferment. My sister and Shlomo had moved back to Israel because after they received their doctorates, Shlomo got a prestigious job at the Weitzman Institute in Rehovot, a suburb of Tel-Aviv. Once again, my dear sister welcomed me into their small apartment, now also inhabited by their toddler, my nephew Gil—*not!* In Israel, I worked on a dairy farm and at the Biblical Zoo in Jerusalem where I met and shacked up with Aviva, a fun American student at the Hebrew University. We ended up living together in her dorm room, and we traveled around Israel together, exploring the various biblical sites and er, doing stuff on the beaches. There are poems here about my experiences in Israel and poems related to my later travels in Spain, Greece, and other parts of Europe after I left Israel.

My main Berkeley girlfriend Bonnie then joined me in Europe, and we took a mime course together in Prague (still under Soviet occupation) with the famous pantomime and actor Fialka. We ended up living in Amsterdam for a year, another hippie mecca. I was writing poems throughout this period too, included. Back to the U.S. and adventures in LA, then returned to Berkeley again. Took off a year later on another ship, a bulk grain carrier (forgot her name) out of the Port of Baltimore. This was an existential time of aimless wandering for me, and I finally ended up in a traditional yoga ashram in Pondicherry, South India where I received my formal yoga/meditation training after 3 months. I also studied with my first guru, Dr. S. A. Ganapathy. Poems from those travels are also herein.

I returned from India to my parents' home, now in Riverdale, the fancier part of the Bronx with a view of the Hudson, where the Kennedys had also lived. My skin color was bright yellow from the Hep A that I had contracted in India and my mother almost fainted when she opened the apartment door and saw my sick, exhausted and scrawny body standing there.

And yes, the FBI had called my long-suffering Etan parents several times, looking for me. I finally had to appear at the induction center downtown on Whitehall Street, which I did. Out of the 100 naked boys there for induction examination, each carrying their own personal folder, I noticed that my folder was the only one with a red tag on it. I enquired with one of the officers why that was. He said, "Cause you're going to Ft. Dix this afternoon." *Fuck!* I freaked out and yelled and demanded to see a psychiatrist. Finally, I got to a shrink's office, and I started stomping around the room, and I told him all kinds of shit about me having to finish my homo porno movie with my bitch boyfriend in SF and shoot up LSD, etc. A great theatrical performance, if I do say so myself, though I was really panicked and desperate at this point too. By the Grace of God, the shrink was a Jew. And Jews generally recognize each other. He looked me straight in the eye for a long time after I had finished ranting and he said, "OK, Boritzer, you're not fit to serve." It got to be lunchtime and all the boys were leaving the building to get some food, and the officer at the door said to me, "Boritzer, you don't need to return." I got my 4F and never looked back. *ThankyaLordy! ThakyaLordy! Baruch Ha'Shem! Thank you, Lord Jesus and Mother Mary! Allah hu Akbar!*

It was 1974 and I stayed in the city for a few months and partnered up with Michael Owens the chef/owner at the East West Café in the East Village. I was happy in NYC, living with my Aunt Gretel and her husband Zwi at their really nice 16th Street and 5th Ave penthouse, working in a great kitchen, and teaching at one of the area's earliest yoga studios in Jersey. During this time, I also published *A Sampler*, included in this collection, along with my weird line drawings. That booklet sold really well, especially on the steps of the Metropolitan Museum *("Hey, real NYC Village poetry here!")*. I not only taught yoga at the Jersey studio, but I also allowed myself to be seduced by two unhappy housewives in my classes.

One fine Sunday afternoon, I showed up to work at the restaurant, and a very black, smokey grease fire was in progress with fire engines and firemen deployed there on our street. The restaurant was completely destroyed, and I decided to head back to Berkeley. Conveniently, one of my bad yoga gals and her husband had decided then to move to Northern California with their two small daughters in order to save their marriage. They needed another driver for their van and car, and along I went with them. Uh, that was a rather sticky situation (literally). Interestingly, my other yogini lover also moved to LA to try to save her marriage. We hooked up there and there are poems about both of these two great ladies in this collection.

In the mid-70s, I decided to clean up my act and look for "a real job." I cut my hair and beard, except for a stupid mustache I kept for some reason. No, I was not going gay. In fact, at that time, I managed to get a job as the Saturday night cook at a swinger's ranch called the Circle S in Walnut Creek. Uh, I really can't get into those details here. I tried selling Encyclopedia Britannica door-to-door and that didn't work out well at all, though I did learn some valuable salesman's techniques that have helped me in my later ventures.

Around 1979, in my efforts to become a bona fide adult, I moved from Berkeley across the Bay to SF, an entirely different world. I managed Francis Coppola's famous Wim's Café on Kearney, did more theatre and also films, and finally, I got my precious SAG card (Screen Actors Guild) with a few lines in *The Right Stuff*. I wrote more poems and at that time I wrote my (now) first bestselling kids' book, *What is God?* which started my whole *What is?* series, now published in 17 languages. I also completed Diogenes, a one-act, one-man play about the historical Greek Cynic philosopher. I found an older actor to play the role and was able to get it produced on KPFK radio in Berkeley, an NPR affiliate station. I may include that in this collection, not sure yet as I write this intro.

Interestingly, my spiritual yogi self and my hungry, worldly material self have lived side by side within me all these years after my India experiences, but not without some inner conflict. I also wrote, starred in and produced my first feature-length film, *Golden Gate*. It was about an out-of-work actor in San Francisco who gets in trouble doing some unsavory acts, nothing biographical, of course. This 16mm effort was a disaster, and we could never sell it which is why you will never find it available. Throughout this period, I also continued writing my poems. Finally, in 1980, I moved to LA to pursue Hollywood stardom.

Well, that's the short explanation of what this book is about. I decided to publish the poems because I think they still hold up. OK, some of them are juvenile, rebellious, and weird. And some of them are Pulitzer contenders! But remember that youth is about self-discovery, ideals, betrayal, and vitality. Have you forgotten? Ha, maybe this collection will bring a smile to your face and spark some memories of your own youthful and creative moments!

Juno Beach, FL 2024

Etan, the little playground terror. The overturned carriage, the stick, the defiant look. Jeez! I would run away too if I saw this kid come into the playground!

On a rainy September day, in 1955, we arrived at the Port of New York from Genoa aboard the Italian luxury liner Andrea Doria. She was a new ship but unfortunately, she was struck by a Swedish freighter off the coast of Cape Cod the following year and sank. I am still wearing my cap from the previous night's Captain's Party. My sister Yael took the photo. I was 5 years old and she was 11. My parents must have been exhilarated but I was just a dumb kid on a big ride, what did I know?

I was naturalized in 1961. At the citizenship exam, I could name three American generals: General Motors, General Electric, and General Mills. When we arrived, I did not speak a word of English. No matter, they just threw me into kindergarten, sink or swim. No ESL then! My parents only spoke their native German to me at home, not Hebrew, so I forgot the mother tongue. But I became fluent in German, despite always answering my parents in English at home. If we had remained in Israel, would I have become a famous Israeli hack? My language skills came from my mother's Rosenthal side of the family.

Needs improvement in self control.
Needs improvement in self control.
[Mrs. Rubin needed to know that there is a hyphen in *self-control*. Wade Jr. High, 1963]

If Mrs. Rubin only knew what was really lurking inside that 17-year-old! My McBurney studious self, around 1968. Blue blazer gray trousers, dark blue tie and white shirt (no stripes!)

Not a happy undergrad. I did not want to be in college!

My early hippie persona. My look then was somewhere between a Hasidic Jew and early Charles Manson.

For all the academic energy and political commotion, Berkeley was also a good place for backyard gardening and occasional afternoon meditation.

I always loved Carlos Santana! And his look. I'm pretty sure he saw me rocking out to Soul Sacrifice when he played at Woodstock and he definitely winked at me.

Jeez, I guess that's what I looked like stoned in those daze in my second McKinley Ave apt, a cool attic unit. We still all had to use the hallway toilet and shower but when you're a 19-year-old hippie, who cares?

The textured cover stock was raspberry red with black font. The elephant thing came out of some reaches of my creative mind. The inside pages were pale yellow. Very psychedelic!

© Etan Boritzer, 1969
2118 McKinley Ave
Berkeley, CA 94703

Just a small old man

standing in the leaf littered friday fall

a four o'clock sun not evening not afternoon

jaw unhinged body frozen aimed forward

draped in journey brown

watching

two boys on tricycles.

lost

as the page turned

i lost it

in a pit of quick refelection

past, when

back then

an old hen

took on ten

quite often

in her pen

whoops

in the Gobi desert

a ship slips by........

green sheep pastured

against sparked blue ocean sky

foam ringed coast rock

pure joy

and then here once more

because its here

the spider cables trunk to trunk

shimmering in filtered dust more sun

and some words heard

bury me in the earth

and plant a tree for me

so the road swept quickly be

to reveal the four lane concrete

for us to dive in

to live in

but never die in.

all pointing to the speck nature
laughing at universals
at you and me at i and them
perhaps a step in back or front of us
you agree on insanity the multirole
you agree that to be free
is to relax and contract
to flutter pulste and concentrate
to emanate and recieve
you see that there is no hope
and no failure
and that layer and layer
of delusions are frosted upon us
by ourselves
whom we must love and despise
you know that pleasure
and laughter ecstasy is the feature length
and that hilly topped observation posts
serve none but the vain fool inmates
are you a prisoner
are you free
yes or no only

I've often thought about dying on the bowery
I mean just dying one night
drunk
on the sidewalk
without a shave
a couple of holes in my shoes
Someone would propably come and get me
after a while
throw me on thee junkpile
Here's another one for ya sam
all rusty and dead
I used to want to donate my body to medicine
but i read somewhere there was an excess of cadavers
Have a cadaver
no thank you, i've already had one
Someone told me they give you 400 dollars
and put a stamp on your fool like
in case of expiration
please forward to
NYU medical center, Bellevue
postage guaranteed
but now the bowery seems a better place
Someone said it costs a lot of money to die
with a funeral and a tombstone and flowers
Who needs it
the bowery is good enough

a flower of the street

(who hasn't)

the world tour and

a 22 hit intellectual blowout

the red haired light

slips through vision's grasp

a slow avenue

a wisp word

she follows a breeze

knowing gales

bare to the glass

an energy of reception

in and out of reach

This bright morning i ask myself questions of noyes importance
the formation of words
the invention
the usenonuse nonsense all relativeness
coming down to a mere thousand inquiries
which for measures and controls beyond my nose
i need to grasp
to answer the endless why
why
depending on how you ask it.
So goliath is dead
shot in the act
fingers taped or not
they didn't give the bitch goddess
much time to realize it
what with the coroner's inquest
splitting friends
parents who don't know a son
which ones do
a cousin pays for the funeral
the goddess tried to figure out
the giant's pants size and his birthday
the philosophical boxer dead too
doped in a car fire
and the fat lady's grandmother
the cretan's inner convulsion after
we played stickball in the schoolyard
and the ravaged skinned rag

The associative thought process
no treatise- pure bellshit
find out for yourself
control the experience
or be part of it
or out of it
many alternatives
decisions, decisions
they keep you busy
in the city
but plese
let's not repeat ourselves too often
in the same manner anyway
so it certainly is a thin line
but trust along the way
chance, fortune
trust the senses
recieve return
be strong courageous
actions of wisdom
and kindness
most people need it
are you a giver or a taker
or both
listen to yourself
what are you saying
what are you thinking
thinking, thinking, thinking

Stopped at the checkstand
for a can of sardines
he made me opne my bag
nothing and nothing
check check two more customers
ok let's have a closer look
(U,S customs again)
absolutely nothing visible

next day being no money day
i reach in for a handful of pennies
he nods as i'm nex in line
check check check 94 cents
i've got some pennies for you
set them down
check check check another customer
10 20 30 40 50 60 70, eighty -four
(he's fast)
i've got four cents stamps
and five makes 93
uh oh
why don't you leave an egg
sur(fumbling)e
never mind
(even)

wht's this at my feet

a drunken dizzy bee

get off the sidewalk

get a grip on yourself, bee

must've just finished

a private jar for

some wealthy grasshopper

who doesn't know the difference

between vintage avocado and alfalf

honey anonymous

probably has fiends

that get together

under a shady tree sometimes

to test flapper flasks

pretense of course

but richer than assembly workers

at rudd

no queen

professional pride

just some of the collection

and a little buzzing

It was really funny.

They had gone to a skin flick

and sat behind an old lady.

About the time they got restless

one of them gurgled

and spat on her neck.

Sitting on this morning bed

listening to the paper wall

moans and ohs of

next door Steve and Beth

me gettin a hard on

her almost cry screaming

him huffing it down

she must have hit the cieling

he must have come

i must have her

silence

the organ church cue

what, then why, then how

or maybe why what how

or how what when

certainly there is a pattern

watch the order of events

try to see the next step

or don't try

words

use the ones you need

but don't fail to express yourself.

A face a face

two eyes a nose

lips and chin

bone and flesh

tis a disgrace

you can't see more

in a face.

A frog once alighted a new pond
the old was too small so he moved on
the others didn't even notice he was gone
perhaps they thought he'd gone to the john.

and so i asked the great prophet
(safe in his mushroom cloud, of cours
what is truth and what
(at this he frowned)
is it that captures me
but elludes at the same time
(he inhaled noisily)
what is space
and what is time
(a small smokering drifted to the sky
Yes and who is it that causes death
(are you listening)
and what of when we know
(the fog thickens)
where are you going
(mysterious isn't it)
yes, but hey, hey prophet

ha

norma jean walked in yesterday

in her gatsby outfit

driving across the wasteland

she plays the starlet but hides the child

or rather doesn't hide it or does

letting men conquer her

though she wins every time

are we destined to the neutrality of it all

or do we bungle and splash

in the changing harvests

for art's sake

and what about the greensilkpantspinkknit pimps

driving their hogs up to the house next door

to check on business

and the beard asking me

the moustache serving me

and illusionary starting blocks

with flower rimmed winner's circles

in view.

The answers are plain

the organization easy

the vision clear

but the path cluttered

and the pilgrim's progress again marked by byways.

I feel like an octopus.

a pattern of the mysterious design

on an ant's antenna

check the appropriate box

or other

is your vision blurred

are you paying attention

and still traveling

the roadsigns are confusing

but the highway is open

find the rest station

where to refuel

and finally home

listen to the madman

crackling fast glaring

sound inaudible to anyone

neither to you nor himself

but perhaps to a child

a frequency of high voltage

of many amps and watts and clearness

the clearness of the white part of an eye

the whitish bluish lake in which swims

a slopp of truth

not listing or drowning

but sailing due north

due direct stright lancing inward

through to the very center

of the feathery luxurious pettiness of

the dog and cat

the supermarket

the school the administrator the past

people in the persons of
the Communist Radio Peking
card carrying old trout
Yup, he said assuredly
and he hammed in every night
which was mor exciting than the FM.(me)
but not more nor less than the
junk pipe skeleton pick up
of the 30-30 law old nail
whose confidence was his
government surveyed Nevada
two or three million tomb
and i told him so
but he knew before me
and had an eleven acre oregon
and the sell-out rig-in eternal
claim claimed
by the no company bullshit
man in L.A. shotgun sure
so we lefthis front yard
smokestack gray shack
and we road by a sand beach
ocean deposit river moss clothed
in a dark treed path of forest
and me i went back an hour
to a glorious infinit sun

At the annual

open the manual

pick a position

heat to proper volition

don't practice alien sedition

nor bear admonition

picnic

I turned to a friend

and said

let's go to bed.

into a Sunday a warm sunday

the faint laughter calls

the sadness the happiness

we must talk we must live

we must have joy

the smile

the crease around the eye

the gaspin stomach of a moment

laugh

we are fools.

I bought my first car in Berkeley, a black 1955 Ford Sedan, for $25. I was hitchhiking in town and a guy picked me up in his old jalopy. I said it was a nice car and he offered to sell it to me for $25. The suspension was ruined and it would shake, rattle and roll over 25 MPH. He drove me to my house, and I gave him the money. Eventually, I needed to go to SF to sell my poetry, so later I bought this 1962 Plymouth Valiant for $300. It had the famous push-button transmission on the left side of the dash. Not exactly a hippie mobile but with the legendary reliable Slant 6 engine. I stopped here at the side of Highway 1, probably to go to the cliffs and watch the sunset. Value today: $32,000.

Bought this 1959 Ford Galaxie 500 Coupe for $200 in perfect condition inside and out. Outside my place on McKinley Ave in Berkeley. Not exactly a hippie mobile either but I was making money at the restaurant. It had 'three on the tree' which was OK in the Berkeley flats. But when I moved to SF, the City of Hills, it was a lot of trouble. I would drive uphill to a stop sign at the top of Jones and Union (a 40% grade) and step hard on the brake. I kept the car in first gear while gently nursing the gas pedal. When I could move through the intersection, I gently released the brake pedal while stepping on the gas, hoping not to stall out, slide backward, and hit the car waiting behind me. Trying to park uphill was even worse. Unfortunately, I had to sell this beauty! Value today, about $45,000.

My second poetry publishing venture. The cover was a medium blue with a red font. *Wha?* Not very readable but nobody told me about proofs in my early publishing career. For this book our graphic designer created the cover in a textured white. The inside pages were gold with blue font, at least readable.

thanks

© Etan Boritzer, 1969
2118 McKinley Ave
Berkeley, CA 94703

Radio listened
direct live in person
from coney island
the side show-
when people looked at her they would gasp
but after you talked to her
she was the most beautiful woman
and you would forget she was
the ugliest girl in the world-
what else could these people do
they'd have to become wards of the state
or dependent on some charity organization-
and his hands would start at the shoulder
that's why we call him the seal boy-
the two faced man, sure
he had two noses
and a third eye in his forehead
but it was blind or dormant-
i remember one night in a hotel room
i was the only able bodied person there
boy did we have a time-
we call her the monkey woman
because she's got hair four to six inches long
all over her body except for hands and feet
and a very nice son
he's got a scholarship to college
right he's got a scholarship-

cont.

WHOOOOSSHHHHH

HUGH HEFNER steps out of his

black leather flying pussy machine

while a drunkard just decided, fuck NIXON-

a woman screams

just because you've got on a uniform

you can't push me

and the peace officer says righttttt-

(UPI) AUDIE MURPHY, who killed or captured

240 germans during WWII was arrested in LAS VEGAS

last night on charges of assault-

did you see a contact lens?

(UPI) "We have to live within the law"

said the millionaire parents of a teenager

in explaining why they had their daughter

arrested for possession and use of marijuana-

did she commit suicide?

no she just died-

you should be more considerate-

(UPI) Graduating students at 15 catholic colleges

throughout the UNITED STATES

have ranked jesus christ

fifth in a popularity poll-

tickticktickticktick tickticktickticktickticktick tickticktickticktickticktickticl

better head for western skies

son

There is a cloud

in the otherways clear sky

it is brashness

which keeps from understanding

it is the mouth

yelling into an ear

on top of the tapedeck loudspeaker

the scream drowning

the rightful whisper

in order to see itself doubly

to keep from the silence

of a hateful self

the aggressor who must constantly stop

to look behind

because he knows

there is no following

you will find him

in the seat

you planned to sit in

push him to a mirror.

I may not be FRANK SINATRA

but when i'm sleeping

in my hotel room

at 12 o'clock in the morning

i don't want to be woken up

by some fireman

trancing up and down the hall

and breaking down my door

with a firehose in his hand

telling me to get out

cause the building's burning-

at least he could give me time

to get a goddamn cigarrette lit.

In pursuit of ecstacy

a deer flits across field

hunter in chase

blade upon blade

slashing quickly by

through tree and tree

sunlight strobe between

second by second

to tire the deer

running strong behind

the catch

a knife into the heart

reds yellows

and then the pull home.

Playland died last night
all the rides closed down
and a drunk pissed behind an empty ticket booth
the taffy and fudge vendor
waited for a child to ask for candy
but ended up watching a load of chocolate melt
the lights of the pinball machine blinked on and off
but no one stopped to play
an old age couple sat on purple chairs
looking at passersby looking at them
in a fading pink greasy spoon
with a plate of left over gravy beside them
no strawhatredstripedjacketandcane man
with his whitelaceruffledressed lady in arm walked by
and the sound of the caliope was missing too
someone said the park hadn't been open on weekdays
before it closed forever
i guess fun isn't only a weekend affair.

Off broadway on broadway

walking down tired streets

hand on cheek

through drunken whore eating crowds

stumbling necktie deaf dumb

slithering in laughter

sneers in every cheers

an ex-pug fighter behind dead eyes

a sister dollar tied to cocks

a child in her arms

as sly big business walks into girlie stores

to rub his nightmare eyes

up and down slick pages

a skirted high heeled man

whose death is his lump

waits outside a hotel

next to a caped flower vermin

spare changed into crawling

sticking out a lifeless hand

(ok i'll say they're only bodies

or perhaps it was another lifetime

or i don't want to bumtrip you

but i can't stop seeing it)

and now a poem—

the acne of the city erupts

beside me, a lamp post.

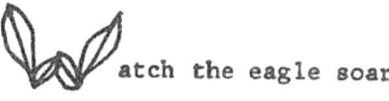atch the eagle soar

alone

sailing winds stately

slowly

into the sky

a sovereign

severe sage

of high ways

feeding the young

atop a mountain

gazing sharp into green sun flashes

waiting for comrade stars

no fear of enemies

and again

a leap

into the downwind

and up.

capable of killing little children
or ruining the happiness of a friend
or torturing someone concerned for me-
i fear pain
and the maiming of myself and others
that tears at the intangible body of images
but more than that
the blood burnt flesh and crushed bones
of screaming men and women
that comes with the misunderstanding of science
and from animals wrenched
of the truth of love and kindness-
i fear not death
for it is a sweet and joyous new birth
but i fear the circumstances
under which the scyth's blade swings
when disease and pain accompany that visitor
scalding the body in flames and nails-
but most of all, i fear myself
for it is through my actions
that i manifest all the horrors of this world
through impurity and selfishness
through action that is false
in the eye of nature and the universe
through unheeded warnings
through short and narrow sightedness
through mistrust
through falling prey to sick impulse

Cup in hand

against a wall

he used to walk stock market halls

but the gold plated street

shined too bright into his eyes

and startled his vision

so that all he acquired was

a shephard collar handle

and a tin rattle

which causes board friends

to forget and look away

while he counts his days

penny by penny.

n the midst of all maybe's

in the midst of was and will be

could be, has been and might have been

come up for a breath of is

refreshing revealing is

everpresent is

which never is for too long

imagine a head spinning from one side to the other

in a coffee parlour adventure series

child and adulthood tales, facts and fancies

or paranoid visions

of family famine and misfortune

if the office/factory fails

listening always to palsy groans

making jerky unsure moves

attached and detached

in and out of the land of is we go

it begins to sound magical even

where is this place called is?

is? never heard of it but when i was in Burma, the summer of '45.....

is? have you tried the phonebooth

is? oh, a marvelous movie

is? i'm not sure buddy but it could be near by

aha- a clue

behind the dresser? near the refrigerator?

am i getting cold or warm?

no, asshole, it is at the end of these words

with the breath that comes

as the eye leaves the printed word..........NOW!

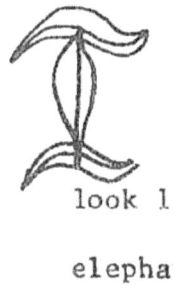   saw a bomb

look like a flower

elephants stampeded

and ants survived

a house stood

one died in heat

i saw laughter and reality

drive a bullet away

a cow chewed slowly

people danced around

an empty soapbox

and the music never ended.

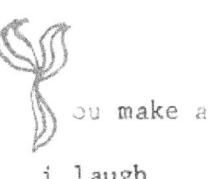
you make a mistake

i laugh

i make a mistake

you laugh

you laugh

i cry

i cry

i see

i see

you see

you see

you tell me

i see

i tell you

we are friends

through my greed to satisfy idiot desire

and malignant jealousy-

i fear only myself

and that which comes out from

this uncontrolled mechanism

and that which comes from

the circular domino theory of life

proved again and again-

that which i do is done unto me-

what else can the parrot reveal

in his well obscured mirror?

the answer is

only more each moment-

but what about you good easy chair listener

what is your fear?

surely i'm not the only frightened person here.

*   *

the echo of a footstep

throughout time

is heard

Admiral Byrd passed by today

(i'll spit in your eye

for looking at me that way)

and he sure looked

helmet raincoat to the ankles cold

but no one knew who he was

though he walked on the gutter side

politely and carefully

i could see he'd been to the poles

but he wasn't recognized

Admiral Byrd

and no one could tell.

What is your fear my friend?
since you won't tell me yours
i'll be skinless enough
to tell you mine, ok?
i fear getting put in a cage
most of all, a steel cage
which police/killers use
like storage freeze boxes
to stop your daily action and thought
the breeding swamp of hatred and violence
which is the slowest death
a man can be sentenced to-
i fear cages in the form
of repetitive thought patterns
my own mostly
getting caught in some mud-hole idea
from which escape would be excruciating-
i fear losing trust
in the forces of the universe
and seeing my own intuition
replaced by some cotton candy god
because that would be disaster
wrought in monsters from the
new york subway system tunnels of darkness
through melting flesh
pressed by sewer fiends of the mind
into devil physical life-
i fear the evil i know
lies within myself

You mean

no it's like

oh i thought you meant

what? uh

well maybe not if you

uh huh

i mean i'm not trying to

you mean

uh

i remember once

yeah that's like

that's a nice

thanks

Twists and turns

a man entombed

in ice

frozen on a mountain

chipped away

by rescue mountaineers

body hard intact

thawed in the handling

strained and wrung

on the plain

and brought to life.

There are some girls

who when you give them love

wear it like an old glove

they spend, squander, exasperate

and flaunt it

until you wonder if you really want it-

what to do in these cases

never ceases to amaze us

but when we do find out

it seems there never was any doubt

as to the thing to be done

and that is simply to get rid of the bitch

and find a fairer one.

i'm the game player

you better play my game

i've got words you never heard of

i've got tricks to make you forget

what you had to say while

i was trying to make you say it

i know how to make you feel bad

like you've been had

i can make what you say

what you are

and i'll take every syllable that you utter

and make it relate to your mother

i'm deep and i can see

that you're trying to hide from me

now you're leaving

you think you've had enough

you're afraid to hear about yourself

you'll never know why and what you are

you don't like to take part

you won't stay and fight it out

you don't like to spit and shout

i know

i'm the game player and i know

so if that's the way you are

you can straightaway go

you're no fun

you don't want to play

well just for that go away.

   could be walking down a street

and see you with your precious fine looks

walking at me

and i may say, hmmm

there's a lovely woman

but then i look up in time

to see a sign that says

salami

and i get the significance

in time to look down and see

a policeman help some crazy old lady

across the street giving her directions

and i say

that's the way my look should be

and i know if we want to

we'll do more than

just look.

Loose man

smokin down the highway

got problems of your own

but they aint showin

dont cry stay high

we re all gonna get by

why worry about that

stick with what we got

everythings allright

we'll get a ride tonight.

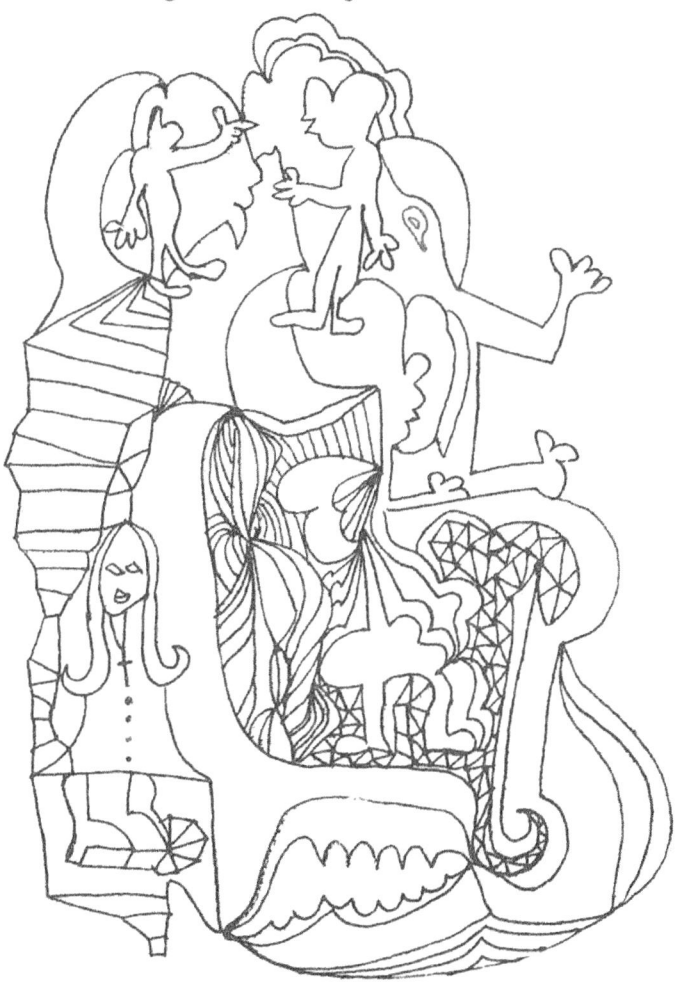

Pondicherry, South India

This authentic jungle saddhu came to visit the ashram one day. A saddhu is a religious ascetic and mendicant who has renounced the worldly life. There are still thousands of these guys wandering around India as they did 5000 years ago. He didn't speak English but knowing what he was, along with his smiling eyes and fluid contortions exhibition, he was quite a unique experience for us Western kids.

Dr. S. A. Ganapathy

In the summer of 1971, I met Dr. S. A. Ganapathy at Gitananda Ashram in Pondicherry, South India where I was residing and enrolled in a 3-month course in traditional yoga and meditation techniques, and yoga philosophy. Dr. Ganapathy showed up at the ashram one day to give us an overview of homeopathic medicine. There was a vibe between us, and he invited me to his small clinic in town.

I started going there regularly and he asked me to bring him some coffee and a pack of cigarettes whenever I visited. He served as an officer with the British in India. He was tall and handsome, with a commanding look and demeanor. He was married to Mrs. Ganapathy and they had two grown sons at the time. He was an enlightened being but very under-the-radar. The big guru deal was down the road at Aurobindo Ashram and he didn't want any part of that Western circus.

He would drink his coffee and smoke his cigarettes while we talked. He would start our sessions with, "What do you want to talk about?" Of course, I wanted to talk about spiritual matters but I also wanted to talk about sex. He knew a lot about both subjects and he discoursed at length to me about them, and other matters. This formal photo is from our time together then.

I returned to Pondy in 1990. Dr. Ganapathy's son Nanda had written to me that if I wanted to see him alive again, I should come sooner than later as he had a series of heart attacks and he was 90 years old then. He moved a bit slower but he looked great. I cried a bit when I sat down next to him. Not he. He just started in on me as if we had sat in his office the day before. I didn't like what he told me about my life during the past 20 years but I knew that he was right. We spent a great week together, digging deep. He gave me some scary practices to do at night in my hotel, which I did. And they were scary.

After I was to leave Pondy, I was headed to the holy northern city of Varanasi on the Ganges and nearby Allahabad for the big Hindu Kumba Mehla festival that is held there every 12 years, with an attendance of 10 million people. Notables like the Dalai Lama, Julia Roberts, Richard Gere and lots of Bollywood stars also fly in. He asked me why I was going there. I said, "Because it's the Kumba Mehla!" He said, "You won't learn anything there."

The day I left, he reached under his mattress and gave me a copy of Carlos Castaneda's *The Fire Within*. I was shocked that Castaneda's book had reached this small town in South India and that Dr. Ganapathy even had it. I asked him where he got it. "Oh," he said casually, "Somebody gave it to me. You should read it."

Dr. Ganapathy passed away peacefully the next year. Nanda informed me. It took till his passing for me to finally sit down to read the book my guru had given me. That restarted the fire within me. I sold my successful art gallery in LA, started working on my kids' books series again, returned to publishing, and got back seriously on my spiritual path.

Dr. S. A. Ganapathy. My first guru and most influential spiritual teacher. *Thank you!*

My third and final effort in street poetry sales after my return to NYC from my draft dodging European sojourn. After this publication, I just starting scribbling down the poems on a pad I always carried with me. That collection starts after this last booklet.

© Etan Boritzer, 1969
2118 McKinley Ave
Berkeley, CA 94703

thank you!

A SAMPLER

by etan boritzer

An Excerpt From One of the Restored Manuscripts Recently Uncovered at the Excavations of Darbey Hut on Dell

Me nimes Anew Agud ov Roy
Ey snitched th Rowll ov Badrad Hoy
Ey kom to sed upon yor bed
An yop th Yope ov Reeni Fred
Nau Mum Mum Mum Be Mum
Mum Mum Mum
Sleep Devi Sleep
Ey Agud's at yor sleev.

A SAMPLER

© copyright May 1973
by Etan Boritzer
and Metaphysics Press
156 Fifth Avenue
New York, New York 10011

contributions
toward cost of publication
are welcome.

Spring

Then comes summer
not spring
one day
suddenly

all candles and lightbulbs appear dim
the harbor smell sticks two fingers in your nostrils
and pulls you out to sea
to unfossil

the old ones emerge
like turtles from the shell
the air gives suckle anew
to each man infant again

you walk easy
from crouched winter
sit with schoolboys
outside the schoolhouse
refusing to go in

you quit the job
shout aloud!
jump into the air!
again all is possible!

all!
all is possible.

Early Christmas

This year
solace comes
like Christmas
too early
and prepackaged

or
like an old friend
gone Jesus –

(please
come and save him
quick).

Where Clothes Hang

The sky puffs
pinto ash and brown
a man's clothes
brought to his house

the beloved waits
while garments are put on
put away

and a man looks not
to his life
only to where his clothes
will hang.

But Sometimes

But sometimes
through the small wanderings
and configurations of ant-like existence
i awaken to the premise of Bigness
and am able for a short time
to distract myself into all manner
of intimate and generous understanding
of this region, Life;

anything may trip the wire
along a line of unseen circuits
and suddenly all becomes immaculate
and clear
suddenly i am bold
and glad
and i feel as if any living thing i pass
could reflect this newborn happiness
back to its source

but it is a fragile happiness
and i guard against the zealot;

these moments come
like water in a sparseness
a short repast

i drink
and am on my way again.

In the Weeds

Late at night
rearranging scenes
from pieces
of a broken egg shell

darts slung inaccurately
bounce off their targets
and further crack
the circle of unsettled minds
sentences trail off dimly
into the blue morning
and a mist surrounds companions
scattered incoherently

in the weeds.

Paradise, a Paradox

Paradise

turned to paradox;

there i was

under the palms

the sky clear and clean

the water blue and warm

but i had come with the wrong person –

myself.

CHEATED

Love

made to stand on its head

scolded

and scowled upon

miscarried

and demanded of

soon bursts

like a fever

and ends

as it did

from the beginning –

cheated.

The Unwilling Sentry

Shadows
in breath shades
of night
sail over half closed eyes
and settle squirmy
into cramped corners

sleep stalks
impatiently
about the room

two slip through time
one at restless watch

and night
climbs a long ladder
into day.

Returning from living in India on a dollar a day (1971), I ensconced myself with my Aunt Gretel (my Mom's older sister) and husband Zwi in their cool penthouse on 16th St and 5th Ave. My mom Lotte is hugging me, sister Yael and her boys Gil and newborn Ariel. The best sister I could ever have asked for!

Dad, Mom, and Gretel. The two most influential women in my life, my mother and Gretel! My mom is proudly holding a copy of my new poetry booklet. My dad George could be tough but he saved my dumb ass numerous times. He loved to kid around, especially with women, but he was always madly in love with Lotte. Worked his butt off for us as the foreman at his brother Max's big outdoor scrap metal yard, in blistering summers and freezing winters, in the South Bronx.

Gretel and me. I could confide anything to Gretel. She gave to me unsparingly and from every perspective; psychological, cultural, historical, financial. Her British sense of humor was always quite sharp and biting. She was the top jewelry enameller in NYC—the top! And she loved her cigarettes and gin.

Zwi Russ was the most creative jewelry designer I have ever seen, even to date. His rings, pendants, necklaces, and bracelets were always hip, modern, witty, beautiful and very unique. They sold everywhere, from Tiffany to Bergdorf, B. Altman and Sak's. He gave my mom some gorgeous pieces—gave!

Jerry's Kids! Remember those long Muscular Dystrophy Association Labor Day telethons that Jerry Lewis hosted for years with tears in his eyes to raise money for these kids' wheelchairs and various programs? MD usually affects boys in early childhood and people with the condition typically only live into their 20s or 30s. I volunteered for two weeks at their summer camp in Warner Hot Springs, CA (NE of San Diego) in 1972.

Each counselor was assigned one kid. I can't remember my kid's name but he was 17 years old and had a good sense of humor so we had a lot of fun floating around in the big 104° sulfur pools and doing the various camp activities. The reality was that a girlfriend of mine had volunteered there and she convinced me to sign up too. Well, despite my romantic motives, I guess I got a few karma points for volunteering. Anyway, we had our own fun after hours.

The cab companies would hire anyone to drive in NYC!

Meanwhile, back in Riverdale. I think I borrowed my dad's hat for this one.

Aunt Gretel always said, "Kleine Etan can do no wrong." Yes, my mom spoiled me and during my drug years we had a tempestuous relationship, but she never gave up on me. I do have some regrets and one of those happened when she was 90 years old and in assisted living in Tucson AZ. where my parents moved in 1986. I took her out to a nice Thai lunch (our last time together) and after we ate she asked me to go over to Safeway and buy her a pack of cigarettes. The fucking cigarettes and her smoking in bed at home at night when she was on Oxycodone and burning holes in her nightgown was why my sister finally decided that she could no longer be trusted to live alone. There was no smoking in the facility, and I refused to buy her that pack of cigarettes. I'll only smoke one, she pleaded. Now I regret denying a dying woman her last cigarette. Ha, she was free-spirited and feisty till the end!

My original Velobind edition! I found an older actor to play the role of Diogenes and it was produced on a local Berkeley radio station in 1979. Diogenes was purported to live in Athens (412 – 323 BCE) during the time of Plato, Aristotle and Alexander the Great. He was a student of Antisthenes, the founder of the Cynics School of Philosophy. The only information on him comes from Diogenes Laërtius' book *Lives and Opinions of Eminent Philosophers*, written c. 330 CE, nearly 600 years after Diogenes' death. I took some episodes and writings from this obscure text, and added my own contemporary twists. Enjoy!

Diogenes the Cynic
Διογένης ὁ Κυνικός

©Etan Boritzer 1979

Diogenes the Cynic

Διογένης ὁ Κυνικός

Etan Boritzer

Complete darkness on the set. Objects are heard being moved noisily about. Snorting, low mutterings, curses not quite intelligible are heard. Upstage a flashlight is lit and moves in a disorderly manner toward the audience, a hand and face become visible. It is Diogenes, hair matted, uneven speckled beard, eyes glaring, a face lined with intelligence and arrogance. A dim blue stage light begins to reveal the entire strength of the figure, disheveled, wearing an overcoat several sizes too large, barefooted, a staff in one hand, the flashlight in the other. He comes close to the audience, shines his light into the faces of individual audience members, viewing one, then another and another, shaking his head in disapproval, muttering, perhaps mimicking the responses. Finally, in exasperation, he shouts:

> I am searching for a man!

He continues searching, and addressing individual audience members,

> I am searching for a man! Are you a man? Man or beast? Man or child? Are you a man?

Threatening with his staff, he looks wildly about. Again he shouts,

> I am searching for a man! Is there a man amongst you? I ask for men and scoundrels gather. A crowd assembles but few who could be called men!

At the top of his voice,

> I am searching for a man!

No response. He looks about, peers into the audience. Silence. Then,

> Why? You ask yourselves, why am I searching for a man? Why not ask why wolves attack sheep, why falcons hunt rabbits, why dogs howl at the moon?

> I am searching for a man because I am Diogenes, Diogenes the dog, the dog who has lost his moon in the glare of the sun!

He howls,

> Owwwwwwww! Owwwwwwwww! Owwwwwwwwwwww!

More blue light comes up slowly. He continues:

> Really, even in the middle of the night, the question, "Why?" immediately invites contrivance. Does a tree ask itself "Why?" Does the sky ask itself "Why?" Does a dog ask itself "Why?" Why should I, Diogenes the Cynic, which for your sake, Bulgarians, means dog, why should I ask myself "Why?" And if I ask myself "Why?" then who is it who answers? Who is it who asks? You see, pure Sophistry. Anyone can do it.

Lights have come up fuller now. The famous tub of Diogenes is revealed surrounded by Doric and Ionian rubble along with old newspapers, tin cans, a clock, a beat-up umbrella, a car grill, every and any sort of junk available. Diogenes puts the flashlight in his coat pocket, picks up a crust of bread from the ground, chews, paces back and forth along the length of the tub and begins mockingly to expound.

> No, it is more important to inquire as to how Diogenes became a dog. Was it poverty which made for the necessity of a dog's existence when Diogenes first came to Athena? Yes. But did Diogenes come originally to Athena to lead a dog's existence? No. Then why and from where did Diogenes originally come? Diocles says that the father of Diogenes, Hicesisus, a banker and native of Sinope, was accused of adulterating the coinage of some public funds he had been placed in charge of and was thus exiled, his son accompanying him. However, Eubilides relates that it was Diogenes who, while in charge of the same workmen, was

himself urged to alter the coinage. Diogenes went to the Delian oracle to ask Apollo whether or not to do as he was asked. The oracle replied that Apollo gave him permission to alter the political currency but Diogenes, failing to comprehend the true meaning of the oracle, proceeded instead to alter the state's coinage. When found out, he was banished, his father accompanying him.

Chews bread thoughtfully, then laughs.

Why, just yesterday, someone tried to reproach me again by saying that the people of Sinope had sentenced me to exile. I answered, "Yes, and I have sentenced them to home-staying." I am even considered of a lowly birth because I am not a true Athenian, but to my mind, a native birth does not give an Athenian more standing than ants or snails born in the same city. And when Lysanius, son of Aeshrio, accused me of having previously been a counterfeiter, I replied, "Yes, then I was such a man as you are now, but such a man as I am today, you shall never be." Ha! That shut him up.

He stands gazing into the tub. He picks up a stick and begins knocking and kicking things in all directions.

When I first came to Athena I determined to correct my interpretation of Apollo's oracle, and so I went directly to Antisthenes, who had the reputation of being a man. I went to the gymnasium of the White Dog, Cynosarges, where he used to converse, and I asked to be accepted as his student. However, it was the habit of Antisthenes to discourage students by beating them over the head with a wooden stick until they fled. When he began the customary initiation, I stood still until my head splintered his cane; then I said, "Strike again, for you will never find wood hard enough to keep me away from you so long as I think you have something to say!"

He breaks the stick then rubs his head.

> Was he a man? Antisthenes was more than a man. He lived in Pireus and every day he walked to Athena and back, five miles in each direction, solely for the purpose of hearing Socrates speak. He was no craftsman or merchant or landowner who could not afford to tearhimself away from his livelihood in order to hear wisdom that had nomonetary value. Yes, he was harsh with himself, and he was harsh with his students also. When asked why, he replied, "Physicians must be harsh with their patients."

He pauses thoughtfully. Then:

> Once someone told Antisthenes that men praised him highly. "Why," he asked, "What have I done wrong?" He disdained praise and friendship alike. He used to say that it was better to fall in with crows than with friends because the former devour you when you are dead whereas the latter devour you while you are still alive. Therefore, he held no one as friend but because of the simplicity of his life and teachings, he attracted many from the lower classes. Thus he was often accused of keeping lowly company. To that he replied, "Physicians also attend their patients without catching disease." And when he heard once that Plato was scorning his methods, Antisthenes remarked that it was the privilege of kings to do good and be ill-spoken of." Asked the highest point of human achievement, Antisthenes declared, "To die happy." Asked what profit he had derived from philosophy, he replied, "The ability to converse with myself." He used to remind men that by definition, philosophy meant simply the love of wisdom. For him, life and philosophy were one. Much different from that vanity called Plato.

He pulls a small tricycle from the tub and begins to ride around in circles.

> For someone like Plato, philosophy is only a word mill where the hard, rough grain of truth is ground down into a useless, powdery cosmetic!

He stops the tricycle and goes to the tub. He takes a large and full shopping bag out of the tub, and pointing to the bag:

> Why, just yesterday I asked Plato for a few figs whereupon he gave me a whole bagful.

Throws bag aside, and continues to ride in circles on the tricycle.

> With Plato, two plus two equals twenty-two! He never gives as he is asked nor answers as he is questioned. He is like the mathematicians who gaze at the sun and moon but overlook matters close at hand; or, like a musician who tunes the strings of his instrument while leaving the dispositions of his soul discordant.

He stops the tricycle and goes to the bag of figs. He eats a few, then drops the bag back into the tub.

> Plato contradicts and confuses the most elementary issues. I spend days and nights searching for the true man while at his Academy, Plato briskly defines man as a biped and featherless animal! When I heard that definition, I brought a plucked chicken into the lecture hall and declared, "Here is Plato's man!" In consequence, to the former definition was appended, "having broad nails." Indeed Plato's worth is such that one time, when I began to eat some salted fish, the great philosopher complained that I was disrupting his class. I asked how he thought a penny's worth of fish could distract from his enlightened discourse but for some strange reason it did.

He leaves the tub and begins to ride around again on
the tricycle while continuing:

> Antisthenes spoke plainly so that even a slave
> might comprehend but Plato speaks of Idea and
> Form, of a cup and cuphood, of a table and
> tablehood. "A cup will never be anything but a
> cup and cuphood will never be anything but
> cuphood. A table will always be a table and
> tablehood will always remain tablehood." All of
> which is "induced" through his remarkable powers
> of reason.
> "Plato," I say, "the cup I see but I see not."
> "That," he informs me, "is because you have not
> experienced 'pure thought,' as Socrates did."
> "And what is this 'pure thought?'" I inquire.
> "The ability to comprehend that which is
> immutable and eternal," comes the reply.
>
> Whereupon that Aristotle of his leaps up and
> shouts, "But there is nothing that is immutable!
> The eternal is not separate from the phenomenal;
> one contains the other. Idea is immanent in Form
> and Form absolutely necessary to Idea: The oak
> rises from an acorn, the statute from marble,
> the state from man and man from the state! All
> of which Aristotle derives through his famous
> "deductive" method, based entirely upon his
> remarkable powers of observation.
>
> At that point, I retire to my salted fish, while
> Plato hurries to the defense of his Republic,
> which he deems the solution to those morbidcaves
> of his imagination. First, he banishes all
> adults over the age often from his model state,
> then — well, to Hades with that! If you want to
> waste your time, read it yourselves. As for me,
> the only true commonwealth is that which is as
> wide and as deep as the Cosmos itself, and mean,
> wrangling minds like those of Plato and
> Aristotle will never comprehend that immensity.
>
> As to the gods, I remember Lysias the druggist

once asked me if I believed in them. "How can I avoid believing in them," I replied, "when I see such godforsaken wretches like you all about me."

He stops and throws the tricycle aside.

   All the supposed reasoning, proofs by limited observation, predetermined conclusions, useless research, and statistics—all based on convention and self-serving motive. All the supposed knowledge gained, all the imagined purposefulness, all misinterpreted, misused, never leading to the one real virtue in this world—wisdom!

He pauses, then:

   But no, none of it troubles me. It does not trouble me, as it did Anaximander, whether we originate from the One or the many, or if the Cosmos will at fixed intervals be dissolved to allow chaos to resume, or whether there is any purpose to the chaos we find ourselves born into. It is simply that I despise Plato and those so-called philosophers. I despise them as being thrice human, meaning thrice wretched. I mock and discredit all their grand mental indulgences. I would rather convene and converse with dogs. A good sharp bark and a large toothy bite is what I appreciate.

He tidies up the tub, gets in and, suiting the action to his words.

   Yes, sometimes, I would rather just stay home in my tub, which the good goddess Cybele kindly sent to me through the elements. I prefer to take the double cloak, which Antisthenes invented for both day and night use, and wrap it about myself like so and to hold my breath, like this…

He holds his breath for a long time. After a slow exhalation, while still wrapped in the coat:

> Ahhh. So peaceful in here. I hope to die in such a manner. Let others argue over what is eternal and what is phenomenal or, which came first: The oak or the acorn. Let all their knowledge and reasoning lead them to create newer and more sophisticated philosophies. And let those philosophies help to create and destroy more warring little states and empires. Let thousands—no, millions!—let millions ram their heads against one another. None hit nor get hit harder than I!

He gets out of the tub.

> Really, I must remember to wear a helmet in public. Why, just yesterday, a person in the street kicked me. I was advised by Philiscus to take the offender to court. But if an ass kicked you, would you take him to court? Unfortunately, that ass could gallop faster than I. No, they can build and rebuild over the ruins of past civilizations, they can fight for each other's lands and against each other's philosophies, but men will never realize how greatly they've confused the original mysteries of the Cosmos and how much further away they are from their simple goals than when they first began their pursuit. I have neither patience nor sympathy for the struggles of Lacedeamon, Thessaly or Thrace. Nor for that matter do I care what happens to Thebes, Chaeronea, Persia or Egypt. What do they care for me, other than my enslavement or destruction?

> And I have no solutions for the problems of Athena in the hands of Phillip and his barbarians either. Though if it were in my power, I would do something about the public baths—for after one bathes in Athena, how is one to get clean? Mostly, however, I have the

perfect vantage from this tub. From here I
attack and to here I retreat. But no, I do not
retreat. I never retreat! I fight them all:
Philosophers, slaves, merchants, kings, states,
gods. I never retreat. But when, by their
numbers, they beat me back, I return to this
tub, this tub from where perhaps the only
solution can come.

He gets back into the tub and looks it over
fondly.

No, it does not appear as much but really it is
very comfortable, and seasonal: In the winter I
pack it with snow and in the summer I fill
it with hot sand!

Gets up again, excitedly.

Why? To accustom myself to truth, to hardship!
I will never run or strive to secure pleasure
or safety the way ordinary so-called men do. I
would rather go mad than pursue pleasure and
perhaps that is the reason for my madness.
But why habituate oneself to falsehood? Wealth,
popularity and power dethrone the authority of
reason. Disrepute and poverty are advantageous
to a true man because they drive him back upon
himself, force him to increase his self-
control and purify his intellect of all
external dross.

The gods gave men the means for easy living, but
men now demand honeyed cakes, perfumed ointments
and costly robes. But not I! I lead the life of
a dog with great happiness: All my senses are
alert and quick and my mind is in my stomach.
Not the same stomach which most men have, that
whirlpool over which they squander their entire
vitality, for that or for some other organ whose
demands they need to repeatedly gratify. No,
this is a stomach whose acids devour with equal
ease any flesh, raw or cooked, any bone, rock or
insult hurled at me.

Gets out of the tub and crawling on all fours.

> Like a dog, I fawn over those who give me anything, bark at those who refuse, and fix my teeth on countless rascals in the street every day. At a certain feast table recently, some people kept throwing all their bones to me. Thereupon, I played a real dog's trick by standing on the table and drenching them right there where they sat.

Standing again:

> It is true that I have practiced begging from statues. Yes! In order to accustom myself to being refused!! Begging is not easy and when begging, I have had to wait at times so long for the generosity of my fellow men that I often thought whatever alms I do receive will be used toward my funeral expenses, rather than for bread. Once a man praised another for giving me money. I asked him why he did not also praise me, who was worthy of receiving the money.

> Yes, all men are beggars of one thing or another. One day Plato approached as I was washing some spinach. He said scornfully to me, "Had you paid court to Dionysis, you would not now be washing spinach." With equal scorn I replied, "Had you washed spinach, you would not have had to pay court to Dionysis."

> Another time, I asked a citizen for alms who said, "Yes, if you can persuade me." I told him if I could persuade him, I'd persuade him to hang himself! Someone remarked to me that people laughed at my behavior. My reply was, "And so very likely do asses laugh at their behavior but as they don't care for what asses think, so neither do I."

He takes a toothbrush from the tub and while brushing,

> As for friends, I treat them as I would a money purse: So long as it is full, I hang it about my neck but when it is empty, I throw it away. Therefore I have neither friends nor possessions, both being overly burdensome.
> I once did own a slave named Manes who ran away. When I was advised to pursue him I said it would be absurd. I reasoned that if Manes can live without Diogenes then Diogenes can live without Manes. I once also owned a bowl and spoon but upon seeing a little slave girl eating with her fingers from the palm of her hand, I knew I could do as well. I am asked now which wine I find pleasant to drink. I answer, "That for which other people pay." They ask, "What sort of man do you consider Diogenes to be?" I reply, "A Socrates gone mad!"

He throws the toothbrush over his shoulder and begins some callisthenic exercises, meanwhile:

> Oh yes, all men are beggars. Even Alexander the Great, Dionysis himself. That's right. He came here, to my tub, and tried to bribe and beg me to govern one of his conquered cities. I told him, as I had told his father Phillip, after the Battle of Chaeronea, when summoned for the same task. I said I could not because I would be a spy.
> "A spy?" he asked.
> "Yes," I replied, "A spy upon your insatiable greed!"
> "I am Alexander the Great!" he exclaimed.
> "And I am Diogenes the Cynic," I answered.
> One of his captains shouted for the soldiers to cut out my tongue.
> "I'll speak from the rear," I said.
> "I'll have you killed!" whined the boy.
> "That's nothing great," I said, "A beetle or tarantula could do the same."
> "Are you not afraid of me?" he asked.
> "Are you a good thing or a bad?"
> "A good thing!" he said.

"Well then," I asked, "Who is afraid of a good thing?"

Diogenes lies down on his back, hands folded under his head for a pillow.

"Is there any favor I could grant you?" he asked.
"Yes," I said, "You can step out of my sunlight."
He became angry again and shouted, "Though you are praised as a wise man and a philosopher, in fact I think you are only a pretender to wisdom!"
"Though I may only be a pretender to wisdom," I replied, "that in itself may be philosophy."
"And you will live and die, thus, alone in the gutters? Who will bury you?" he asked.
"Whoever wants the house," was my answer.
"Before I go," he said, "Impart to me one teaching."
"Very well," said I, "But first you must follow me about the marketplace for one week carrying a tuna in your arms."
"What! I am Alexander! I am Dionysis! I will do no such thing!"
"You see," I said, "Already such a small thing as a fish disrupts your education. And though men praise you, Alexander, I will now instruct you on what Diogenes considers praiseworthy.

Listen carefully. Diogenes praises those who are about to marry but refrain; those who propose to rear a family, but never do; those who intend to go on a voyage, but never set sail; those who think to enter politics but turn back before reaching the offices of influence; those who go out to conquer others but instead conquer themselves, and those who conquer themselves but know that the real battle has only just begun. These are some of the things Diogenes considers praiseworthy."
He was silent.
"Were I not Alexander," he said, "I should have liked to be Diogenes."

Then he left to beg for glory elsewhere.

He goes back to the tub.

> Philiscus said I was a fool not to welcome
> good fortune. Illfortune, I say! To march when
> Alexander marches, to dine when Alexander
> dines, to retire when Alexander retires? No, I
> prefer a dog's life.

He fetches a can of beans from the tub, opens it
with a can opener and begins to eat from the can
with his bare hands.

> But then, what philosophy does a dog have?
> Basically this: If you take point A, I take
> point B; if you take point B, I take point A.
> If I am forced to choose between A and B, then
> I choose C. If you say virtue, meaning wisdom,
> can be learned, I say it must be torn away
> from convention. If you say virtue cannot be
> learned, I say not many can endure its
> hardships. If you then ask how is one to
> restrain evil? I reply,
> By wearing, throughout life, a bit between
> one's teeth.
>
> But really, how tedious! Dogs are not really
> interested in argument or discussion. A dog is
> interested in hardship, in developing
> an indifference to cold or heat, hunger or
> discomfort. And this dog is interested only in
> the strenuous practice of mind and body to
> attain a preference for the virtues of wisdom
> over everything else. Wisdom is the greatest
> virtue, virtue means skill, and that skill
> can only be gotten through hardship and
> simplicity. Therefore, I have composed these
> simple lines about Diogenes:
>
>> A homeless exile,
>> to his country dead.
>> A wanderer who begs
>> his daily bread.

But though I claim no philosophy, to fate I oppose courage; to the laws of men, I oppose nature; to passion, I oppose reason! And in reverse: To courage, I oppose fate; to nature, the laws of men and to reason, passion!
I practice this logic by entering theatres head-on, as the crowdspour out, for that is how life is lived by great men.

Pauses, eats, then:

> When I am asked what I have learned from philosophy, I reply, "To be prepared for every kind of fortune!" And as I am certain of my training, I live freely, with great abandon and little regard for consequence, totally self-sufficient. Self-sufficient, how? Because everything is property of the wise. Again, how? Because everything belongs to the gods, the gods are friendsof the wise and friends share all property in common; therefore, all things are property of the wise. Or in plainer words, the man of virtue wants nothing, therefore he lacks nothing, therefore he is selfsufficient. And this self-imposed life of hardship is the price I pay for my independence.

Points to the tub.

> No, Diogenes sees nothing wrong in living in a tub that he "borrowed" from the good goddess Cybele. He sees nothing wrong in eating the flesh of an animal or tasting the flesh of a woman. Everything is pervaded by everything else and therefore it is illogical to abstain from one thing and not the other. I pursue nothing but I welcome whatever fate sends—good or bad.

Reads label on can while continuing the discourse.

> However, there are certain things we should take in very small dosages. Things such as Geometry, Astronomy, Politics and sports, as

they are all useless, except to make ridicule of. Even Socrates maintained that Geometry should be studied only to the point at whicha man is able to measure the land which he sells or acquires. But men love to complicate life beyond their capabilities. Complexity tothem implies great meaning and upon these seemingly meaningful complexities, great arbiters and imposters thrive and perpetuate their own well-being by undermining the well-being of others; all in the name of Knowledge, the gods and the State. Sports develop the body but not the mind. As for the Arts, they only further serve to divert men from the true questions of existence. Art means excellence and where is that to be found today? Were they not watching the overblown tragedies played in the amphitheaters, men might have to contemplate the mindless tragedies of their own lives.Perhaps long enough contemplation might move them to make some striking change. But instead, more and more refuges for the already shallow emotions and intellect of the populace are daily invented.

Eats some more, then:

But no, I don't despise pleasure, though the despising of pleasure can be a great pleasure in itself. Even Socrates, though he held that wisdom was the supreme human virtue, admitted to a certain extent the importance of one of virtue's utilitarian sides, that of making happiness at least a subsidiary end of wisdom. But I am not like Aristippus and his followers who have seized upon that end before even approaching the beginning of Socrates' meaning. And I am not like Hegesias who totally denied the possibility of pleasure in life and advocated suicide as insuring at least the absence of pain. No, Diogenes despises only the pursuit of pleasure, the clinging to and ultimate grief due to the inevitable loss of pleasure; therefore, nine-tenths of what is named pleasure is despicable and pathetic to Diogenes the Dog.

He leans back into the tub, musing:

> Oh, but I have had some great pleasures in life, even here in Cybele's tub. Yes, news of my wisdom and lowliness reached the finely shaped ears of Lais, courtesan to Demonsthenes, the Orator. She came here herself to ask if I preferred the icy embraces of statues in winter to those of a real woman. I replied that in the end there may not be a large difference between the two but nevertheless, she should enter my apartments, and see to which room I lead her. Of course, she wanted, as everyone does, four walls and a roof to conceal her virtue, but when I refused to leave my humble home, she agreed to return that night.

Stretches in the tub, then:

> Ah, it was a memorable evening — for her. It fled my mind completely until the following day, when Philiscus, having somehow heard the news, came to me and asked, "Do you not despise a woman whohas been used so many times before?" I asked him in return, "When you sail a ship, do you care how many have sailed on it before you?" As for love, it is simply the business of the idle. And marriage, for those who think they can escape hardship by it, I believe only in a community of husbands and wives, where the only law is that of mutual consent. As for the children, they should be raised by the father or by some male tutors so that they learn early in life to have strength, courage and cunning in all things.

He laughs, then looks through some tattered newspapers.

No, I don't care for writing any of it down
either. I'll leave that to those too sensitive
to bear the continuous disruptions and
incongruities of life. Socrates, the son of
a stonemason, never wrote and besides,
writing can't teach the love of indifference,
that element which alone subdues all hardships.
Diogenes gets up, paces and begins to harangue:
Indifference! Indifference is not a passive,
fatalistic thing. Indifference is not the
loss of will nor a submissive acceptance of
all the perplexity and idiocy around us.
Indifference means contempt for death, disdain
for what ordinary men call living, a plunge
into danger, recklessness, chance. As nature is
indifferent to birth and death, indifference
means the deliberate daring to fight, to
conquer, regardless of risk or convention. But
instead, men prefer ease and pleasure, small
intellect and again, over and over, the futile
attempts to coax meaning from the repetitious
confusion and pain, to create great and small
differences out of the in-difference of the
Cosmos.

Even such a thing as wisdom or virtue
is a small man-made detail. Yes, had the coins
at Sinope not been altered, and father and I
not exiled, I should never have come to Athena
and learned what I know today. So, what role
did virtue play, what role wisdom? You see, we
think we can make our own destinies, that
we can create life and impose our sordid will
wherever we choose. We believe, as Heraclitus
did, that the sun is no larger than it appears,
that our choices are as they appear in our
minds. No! Our only choice is indifference,
indifference is our only answer to fate, and
that quality of indifference is what steels,
sustains and goads the true man to victory in
the battle of life.

Pauses, then, continues:

> The proof is simple. In times of ease and
> plenty man develops the conceit of a god.
> But let one plague, one drought or any disaster
> appear and see how men fall upon their knees
> and grovel on their elbows, bewailing the gods
> to deal mercifully with their fragile bodies
> and minds. O Zeus, safeguard us against
> discomfort! Protect us from the destruction
> of our reason! No, I cultivate the reason of
> indifference. I do not follow the dictates of
> the ancients, of the moderns, of my own mind
> even. I am but a dog, a rabid dog, who never
> questions his disease, truth. I am indifferent
> to my affliction and am ready to afflict anyone
> fortunate enough to cross my path.

He pauses, then:

> And if men can't understand the reason of
> indifference, with all its contradictions:
> How wisdom is necessary for happiness, how
> indifference is needed to overcome hardship,
> if men can't restrain their evil, let them
> buy themselves a rope and either beat
> themselves with it or spare the state the
> expense of a hanging. It is not life which
> is evil, only men and their small understanding.
> The target in life is wisdom and if men are
> badarchers, the best place to stand is near the
> target.

He sits down on the rim of the tub.

> All these facts I know quite plainly now, and
> I shall keep knowing them until I die at the
> age of ninety. He points to the inside of his
> cloak. Oh yes, I have seen it all very clearly
> in here. Soon I will grow weary of Athena.
> Debate and discourse ultimately do very little.
> Only trauma can cause change in a man's life
> and even then, one can't be certain that the
> new path taken is any less insipid or more
> noble than the old one. Each day becomes a
> little more insane. Why, men are so nearly

> crazy that one word, one finger can create
> chaos. Yes, if you go about the streets with
> your middle finger stretched out like this,
> someone will soon assault you; but if it is
> the little finger, you will only be judged mad
> and no one will trouble you.

He begins to pace.

> Yes, Alexander will be followed by Antigonus,
> Antigonus by Lysimachus, a succession of weak
> and stupid governors until more barbarians
> swing down from the North to destroy whatever
> the Greeks have not already polluted or
> destroyed themselves. A man can only hope
> to better himself; whatever good he does for
> the world is purely by accident.

Stops. Gets in the tub and begins rowing motions, and mimes other actions described.

> Seeking for the first time to escape the
> fate of Diogenes, I set sail for Aegina. Along
> the way, I am captured by the pirate Scirpalus
> and taken to Crete to be sold as a slave.
> At the auction, the crier asks what I can do.
> "Govern men!" I reply. Then I see a certain
> citizen with a fine purple border to his robe,
> standing there with his two sons. "Sell me to
> that man over there," I shout. "He looks like
> he needs a master." Xenides, the lucky buyer,
> takes me to his home in Corinth. Along the way,
> I tell him, "See that you obey me, for even
> if a captain or a physician were sold in
> slavery, still he would be obeyed."
>
> No, there is no escape, no retreat. Fate
> demands obedience; the battle continues,
> only the battleground changes. Again suiting
> the action to the words. I train his sons to
> ride, to shoot the boy, to hurl Javelin, to
> wrestle. As trainers do with choruses, I set
> the note high to ensure that the right one is
> easily hit. I instruct them in history and

> geography and train them to have excellent
> memories. Their hair is cut short, they walk
> barefoot, eat plain foods. We go hunting and
> they are held in great esteem by whomever
> they meet.
>
> A certain Athenian wants to ransom me out of
> slavery but I say to him, "Don't be a fool, for
> lions are not the slaves of those who feed them
> but rather those who feed lions are
> the slaves."
>
> I grow old in Xenides* house. Students gather,
> again I take up discourse and debate, at the
> Gymnasium in Corinth. People say to me, "Rest,
> you are old." And I reply, "What? If I am running
> a race, should I slow down before the finish
> line?"
>
> Xenides asks one day how I wish to be buried
> and I answer, "On my face."
> "Why?" he asks.
> "Because in a short time, the world will be
> turned completely upside down!"

Diogenes comes to downstage center, again following the action to the words.

> Then, one day, I say farewell to Xenides and
> his sons. I go a long distance into the hills
> and find a warm, sun-filled spot. I remove my
> cloak and sit. One deep breath, I hold…

Pause. Then he falls over, as if dead. Gets up, dusts himself off, puts cloak back on, takes up the flashlight and staff.

> I have instructed them to leave my body out,
> unburied, so that every wild beast can feed
> upon it but instead, they will bury me under
> a tall column of Parian marble upon which will
> stand a white marble dog. As it was my model
> in life, sniffing out every place, person or

> thought I ever passed, tasting every excretion, from the most bitter to the most sublime, as a dog was my tutor in life, so shall a dog instruct me in the Underworld.

Lights come up slowly indicating the approach of daylight.

> Ah, and so it begins all over again. Let me think what form I shall use today. Yes, this one works well: Sir, if you have already given today, give to me also; if not, then begin with me. Do you know why people give to beggars and not to philosophers? Because they secretly fear that one day they too may become blind or lame but they never expect to become philosophers.

Lights have come on quarter full now. Diogenes switches on his flashlight and begins to move around and through the audience.

> I am searching for a man! Are you a man? Man or child? Man or beast? I am searching for a man!

He steps back onstage and exits until we see only the light from his flashlight.

Three-piece, polyester designer cabin crew uniform in some weird rust color. Note the mustache. I had to cut my hair and beard to get the job but I wanted to retain some vestige of my hippiedom past. At the old passenger terminal at Oakland Airport, circa 1975.

Yeah, you had to walk on the runway to get on and off the plane at Oakland in the '70s. We flew Boeing 747. McDonnell Douglas DC 10 (with the elevator down to the galley) and Lockheed 1011. Being a crew member, you really get to know some scary shit about flying in passenger jets.

Airline steward! Big deal, right? Earning $20 an hour back then but that only applied as 'block-to-block' time. It was a lot in those days but didn't include travel time to and from airports to lodgings, etc. The work was grueling, as I discussed in the intro.

What was I thinking? I was thinking that since I still had my designer World Airways 3-piece suit, I could strike some poses and have GQ at my doorstep within days

Of course, no self-respecting hippie would ever purchase or study a GQ but I knew I had the stuff they were looking for in a hot new male model. My dad came out o visit me and being a German-trained tailor by profession before we came to America, he went with me to buy this sharp jacket.

This was about a year later after I moved to San Francisco and thankfully I finally could let go of that stupid mustache. I believe my dad also bought me that nice cream white suit. No calls from GQ at this point but I knew they would come begging for me soon.

I know, I know–*hot!*

100 Poems
Etan Boritzer
© 1979

Etan Boritzer
1025 Powell Street, #32
San Francisco, CA 94108

Table of Contents

Tarragoña...1
What Cares Suez...2
The Ghora, Patmos...3
Naxos...4
Mycenae..5
Point Lobos...6
The Season of Afternoons...7
Antwerp...8
Sailor's District, Amsterdam...9
3rd Ave. and 14th St. NYC..10
Poles..11
Jellal-ed-din Rumi...12
India Landscape, 5AM..13
Lawspet, South India..14
The Diary of Nijinsky..15
In Pursuit of Ecstacy..17
Where Clothes Hang..18
City Poem..21
I Was Not Thinking of Someone...22
Spring (Amsterdam, 1971)...24
A Dream of Frankenstein...26
The Dead Refuse to Die...27
A Wind Burns Hollow...28
From a Painting by P. Maxwell...29
The Unwilling Sentry..30
Strangled Breaths...31
For Gretel...32
Abortive Attempts...33
Night Transit..34
m/v TROPWAVE..41
Seaman's Confession.. 42
A Sailor's Romance..43
Riverdale..44
Chuang Tzu...45
For The Juggler..47
The Door Mime...48

The Painters' Mime	49
In the Forest	50
As Opposites Meet	51
Who Works the Rubber Bridge?	52
Admiral Byrd	53
Water Fugue	59
In the Weeds	61
This Year	63
In a Bank	65
The Scarlet-Capped Black Boy	66
I May Not Be Frank Sinatra	70
One Claim	71
You Know This Place	72
A Bust of Shakespeare Found in the Sand	73
Returning from a Job Interview	74
Cat	76
A Summer Morning	77
On the Runway	78
From a Window Seat, Miles High	80
Landing Approach	81
In a Waiting Room	82
Helping the Artist to Hang Paintings	83
Madame de Pompadour at the Legion of Honor	84
At the Museum	85
Leaves	86
Water Scenario	87
The Poet in Love	89
In Coupled Night	90
The Kiss	91
The Scent of Rain	96
A Farewell	97
The Dilemma of C	98
After the Film	99

Tarragoña

To remember:

a sea of silver molten
mulling over itself

a heat
of fat priestly hands
laid around the neck

the sun, a knife

the bony lap of earth and rock

the town sweating a solar mist
panting in its own reflection

wild herbs rooting in the nostrils

a sky-

his eyelids close
and through their skin
a dancing red screen
a whistle piercing noon

a moment,
he circles it.

What Cares Suez?(1974)

What cares Suez
for the red granite <u>wadis</u>
or tortured skies
of Sinai?

Through the sand-scraped waste
a silver bus vacuums its way,
a radio belches static comments
while the heads of drowsy passengers
roll off their necks.

A soldier's boot,
the mangle of rust,
a village of doorless houses and wind,
dates dry useless on the branch

and not a guest left
to mark the wedding of hate
but Suez, the dead river
knows how to wait.

The Chora, Patmos

"Like something valuable lost in the ocean,"
she grieves before a sealed truth
as cloud hands clamber over mountains-

The walled city
guarding the cave of the Apostle,
the eerieness of a scratched dream
a dark wind searching the cobbled alleys
of shuttered windows and locked doors.
At the taverna the men dance their sorrow
while hostile monks guard a mazed secret.

Nearly summer.
The tourists will soon be coming.
You get up to the monastery by bus
and down, all in one hour.
We have been here two weeks.
What is this place, we are wondering
where icons of grief are painted in the air.

Naxos

Lizard on stone
anxious
staccato

a splotched cow winds a thick purple tongue
around a splash of grass
and yanks it up

rapidly a nanny with bloated teat sac
nibbles to the bald soil

a ewe casually grazes her way over a ledge
and plunges down
to the black rocks and sea

a quiet pastoral,
a witless order.

Mycenae

For the weight of a pin-

the burning falcon
with eyelids sewn shut

the sheep
shorn to their pink flesh

a wind
churned by bees

drops of bright blood,
the poppies

a donkey cry
scraping the boulders-

the sun like a white spider
the skeleton ruins
and maggots bore into the carcass
of a civilization.

Point Lobos

Over the shooting echoes
of fisted waves
Above the skimming sea birds
and the silent brute sweeps
of the headlands' currents
Upon a bare point
Far from self and city
A live figurehead
at the bow of land's end

And the broad
distant
whole.

The Season of Afternoons

Light is a slit in murky clouds
the waves darken
a freighter hovers on the horizon
a small plane drills the air
above the salt sand

the season of melancholy
she reaches across the table for an ashtray
and using some kitchen chrome as a mirror,
she daubs an ashen moustache over her lip
and deepens the shadow beneath her eyes-
we feed slowly upon the afternoon
not yet upon ourselves

the season dampens and folds up
we await a lavender death
night, wherein to rest
but the afternoon will not pass-
where is our hunger?
an ocean prolongs the day.

Antwerp

The room permits
one chair
a bed
a closet
a gray window
facing other gray windows-

on the chair
ablaze
an orange
sustains life.

Sailor's District, Amsterdam

Lurid promises
but no contracts,
you are swept in
by the violet mask of flesh
and its receeding light

from behind a curtain
the agent peers
pistol in hand

and so long you sought
to avoid this end.

3rd Ave. and 14th St, NYC

That tight skirt whore
cool, possessed
one eye for the loveless
one for the police,
that promise
that hope for abandon
suspended forever in shadows—

I pass her late nights
and the desolation leaps out of me
yearning.

Poles

Poles for reference,
yearning and concern-
compulsion for poles
human poles
living's worth alone
at those poles
in strange ports
one reaches back
to well knowns
struggling between falls
and floats
grasping through oceans
and walls
kindred plights and pleasures
home
trees, dogs, certain skies home-

in a storm
I seize any boat!
now that's heaven-cocky,
ain't it, Flo?

Jellal-ed-din Rumi

The vultures have picked the last bone.
Better now to quit the black tent
  of the nomad
And learn the language of lizards
  and stones,
Better the gales of dust and insects
  and the eggs of the spider.
See there—
The lion-colored city hovers sleeping
  above the mist.
At the tomb of the saint
A ghost lays down the prayer mat.
The dead branches of the acacia turn silver—
Why do you tarry?
Have we not pointed the way?
Leave your purse of gold!
They accept no payment there.
Take this mare with the narrow face
  and quick eyes.
Ride hard,
Before the sun loses its way.
Only ride, youth
Ride!

India Landscape, 5AM

The rains have not yet come.
In the blur before morning
blue phantoms squat along the road
and chant quietly for Divine Mother to appear.
Within the huts murky movements have begun,
the red earth is still black.

This night the master has beaten his servant
and discharged him.
Now the man, with empty eyes
lies atop a mound of brown bones.

Oxcarts slowly creak toward the village,
the small bells capping the oxen horns tinkle dully.
One driver, asleep
lets the switch slip frmo between his fingers.

The servant attempts to rise.
The rag slides off his loins.
Two or three stars still flicker in the sky,
dawn exhumes the night.

And the women come in slender saris
picking up with bare hands
the defecations of the beasts,
to be used for cooking fuel and bricks.
Somewhere a car horn is bleating.

The earth continues its eastward spin,
from the horizon of palms a glowing sun is hatched.
The children get on their way to school
and the servant feels no fear,
the rains will come—
Divine Mother will appear.

Lawspet, South India

Time's patient lock breaks in flight
we put down to a clearing
the wings, the voices
all stops

mirror sharp
an instant congeals
an era, liquid
intimate
without confusion of great or small
vast, continuous
all lightly grasp the feathered moment-

then, too eerie
the crystal cracks
the color wheels begin their clamor
and soon we are en route again.

The Diary of Nijinsky

love me I love you love me I love
never understood, never understanding-

the mind retreats,
a dance without legs.

Cobra rising
stiffly
from side to side
he tears with eye of eyes
both sides of face
seen, unseen
smiling
knowing
gleaming
in brilliant heat
devouring
voices of mouse.

In Pursuit of Ecstacy

In pursuit of ecstacy
a deer flits over field
hunter in chase
blade by blade
slashing quickly by
past tree and tree
sunlight strobe between
second by second
tiring the game
a twist
dust swirling
a knife into the heart
reds, yellows reeling-

then the pull home.

Where Clothes Hang

The sky puffs
pinto ash and brown
a man's clothes
brought to his house

waiting
while garments are put on
put away

a man looks
not to his life
but only to where
his clothes will hang.

Dark and bowed figures prowl the night
blurred eyes, suitcases
oily clothes and bared necks-
scant offerings to death's hand.

Men stop
having no place left to go
having hung their fates on the hinge of time-
they swing uselessly back and forth

Ship sit quat and deep
in the black lap of the harbor
laden with mice and lightbulbs-
they await an empty berth.

Those whose hands are holes
whose minds and mouths and genitals are holes
out of which the miles and years leak
and catch like urine in doorways.

Tabriz offered his head as payment
and signed his name on the desert sky-
after he had been nourished,
the assassins came to claim their part.

A documentary in grays and whites
of Nazi armies advancing grimly
into the frozen core of Russia-
grizzled men, black eyed
thoughts and bowels frozen
boots bound in rags
unlit cigarettes hanging from black lips
dead men marching toward further death
Hitler's orders:
not to retreat one centimeter-

Sometimes an army of one
advances in that manner.

City Poem

The sallow sky
the ashen spires
a swelter of vexation
suffocated
into submission—

leaks
from the rusty bottom
apparitions groaning
murder
sperm

a sullen day,
poems trickle out.

I Was Not Thinking of Someone

I was not thinking of someone
like a square and flat brown suitcase
filled with stones
to drag my arm down—

It was on a stroll
through the Sunday city
the ravines dotted with couples and sunlight
when I began to feel
too much alone
needing
just another arm,
I suppose.

In the agitated throats
of others
our minute happinesses
are made
and unmade

bodies that collide
in darkness
groan
in obscure languages,
the void marriage
of terror and hope

indecent
we gather together
homeless
in towns too small
staying too long
with nothing
to feed upon
but ourselves.

Spring (Amsterdam, 1971)

Then comes summer
not spring
one day
suddenly
all candles
and lightbulbs
appear dim,
that foul harbor smell
sticks two fingers
in the nostrils
and pulls you out to sea
to unfossil-
the old ones emerge
like turtles from the shell
the air gives suckle anew
to each man, infant again-
you walk easy
from crouched winter,
sit with schoolboys
outside the schoolhouse
refusing to go in,
you quit the job,
to hell with the landlady-
spring up, shout loud!
again all is possible,
now!

In the Garden of the Planets
fever, no sleep-

over brooding clouds
the ground shows cracks of light

a soldier lurches
into the path of a bullet

a hand clawing for gold and amulets
into a human neck

ashes fall into milk

waves hiss

a penis, glistening red
animal-like

I cannot lure sleep
and already somber dawn approaches.

A Dream of Frankenstein

The vaulted sea walls
the sleepless sea

Frankenstein was chasing me
he only wanted love
to crush me in his arms
to tell me some secret

I must find Frankenstein
perhaps in this subterranean place
he has already found H.
and taken him into his secret
I must open these doors

In the street/above
the villagers are pissing on Frankenstein
they threaten to cook him
in their pots but really
he is wandering around these dark corridors
and H. who vomited blood
when the villagers attacked Frankenstein
has disappeared-

I have to open one of these doors
there is an office behind this door
some people from my childhood are working here

I awaken and turn on the lights quickly
I am very frightened
I think:
Gautama was called The Anchorite
because he was anchored to love
because he had attained the Ten Virtues
I must not be a phantom
I must not lie to people
and cause them to see phantoms
I must tell P. that I love her
that confusion will pass
I must change my life
I must love more
I must find Frankenstein.

The Dead Refuse to Die

Jealous of the sun
they stir the wind
and pretend to frolic therein
yet ever does birth elude them.

The City of Catacombs, Necropolis
is damp and yellow
with the breath of centuries.
The inmates break into the sepulchres
of their neighbors
and the murmuring traffic of pain
never abates.
From the mountainside at sunset,
blood drains into the valley below.
The gatekeeper hears the emaciate howling
but remains unmoved,
the closing hour has come and gone.

And ever do I meet again
those I thought betrayed to time.
Their faces change, their names
but always I recognize them
and always the unfinished business.

A Wind Burns Hollow

Awakening
from a snake dance of dreams
a wind burns hollow
past the hour of mercies

the house shivers
a door is kicked open
lost murmurs
commune with the night air
while a wind like boar tusks
nudges the virgin portal

the skin is hard and cold
and in the field of shadows
a plows turns the soil of seasons
the burnt seed sprouts
and a hole, no longer rectangle
beckons.

From a Painting by P. Maxwell

The pure black and clouded turmoil
of worlds onward, beyond
and immediately beneath
the sordid face of cowardly geometries-

Towering, rumbling, seething shifting worlds
restless vapors reveal
the monstrous grindings and machinations
of whole universes in groping chaos,
darkness glancing off darkness
lubed by the volcanic reasoning of fiery rivers
suns bolt out rebellious from galactic ranks
eclipses and moon shadows born from yet denser shadows,
the hammerings and white heat of the iron forge
the taste of burning friction-

the creation music,
the working god.

The Unwilling Sentry

Shadows
in breath shades
of night
sail over half-closed eyes
and settle squirmy
in cramped corners

sleep stalks
impatiently
about the room

two slip through time
one at restless watch

and night
climbs a long ladder
into day.

Strangled Breaths

Strangled breaths
from behind the wall

terrified
I will not rise
to see who is dying

when confronted
all apparitions disappear

but in sleep
there is refuge-

I seek sleep
only to uncover
dreams.

For Gretel

It sweeps everything
into its looming mouth-

then it vomits everything back
but you.

Abortive Attempts

Like too many embellishments
or like a ventriloquist
and an unresponsive dummy,
or like a string quartet
in the streets with grim drunks
and fire engines all around-

O Mingus.
if we do not lie,
that horrible death
will overwhelm us even more.

Night Transit

Having ground down
the welcome street of eye,
let there be no mourning.

Choice had its choice
over the slate black sea
and the red mists of dawn,
confessed to mannikins
in the whisky light of glass rooms,
played the child long enough
and flew with tin wings
and pulled the ace card, death.

Say now that choice fashioned excuse
for all heroes and phantoms
and anxiously we pray
for those proofs to balance.

At sunset the birds stir a frantic wind
in the brains of trees
overhead, wires buzz heavily, dangerous
with electricity
the city stitches life-lights
into a mournful dusk
everyone flees the day—

I too have planted seeds in this cement
and put eternity aside
but now I want to take off my coat of hours
and go to where the black sun lives
I want to wash the face of night with milk

and later, surfacing from sleep
into a sudden square of silence,
an obscure presence reports:
there is no waking
nor opening of eyes there—

I hesitate
but morning and the Iron Age do not,
arithmetic shapes and sharp sounds
invade the antechamber—
next time,
I will remain behind.

Bears are pawing
the music dark air
performing simple tricks
on quivering hind legs

the trainers
in tight sequin costumes
are splitting invisible whips
mocking with teasing hips
and buttered lips

but the bears want badly
those laughing breasts
the flying hair
and hidden thighs,
the small shoes
and little fingers

because
because
because a bear too
must dream.

It's only the nature of the beast
to growl and show his teeth
to snap at you and bite your knee
to bark and knock you down
to jump on a chair
hang out his tongue and pant
to smile at you
scratch, fall backwards
trot off and not care--
it's only the nature of the beast.

Cat jumps bird
three drops of blood

wings beat against fur
takes it under the house

second bird flies down
nothing to be done
flies away

cigarette smoke
against the window.

The green moon
and she, thin as glass

"through unfortunate events
one is enriched"

hears the skin of night

"if in truth you have faith,
ask not why"

slowly tear

"stability being stronger
than fate"

and give birth

"the past contracts,
the future expands"

to a glass child.

Only what is gray
will survive this grayness
this mountain whose granite teeth
comb back boulder-breathed clouds
and gray snow
under a slow silver eye

my footprints return
to meet those coming up
the silence shifts
behind one pine, then another
I put an ear
to the wall of wind
and try to enter

but my feet are already too far below
and I am running stupidly
to catch them.

m/v TROPWAVE

Death,
his harbor.

They said,
That ass-licker,
he was never around much anyway.

And one day I recall
finding him in the Wheel House
singing, Happy Birthday to me
        Happy Birthday to me.

The Zulu remarked, Mutinous talk
keep away from that one-

And once he said to me,
In darkness
it doesn't matter
whether your eyes are open or shut.

A radio message, Suicide.
And eventually the whole business disgusted me.

Seaman's Confession

Those English whores in Durban
the Syrian in Piraeus
dry dock, the wife and kids in Rijeka
Haifa, and riding ballast to Baltimore
soya and corn back to Rotterdam,
misfit seamen know the earth is round
and there is no escape-
Like drunks and prisoners
they blame everything else
but in the end a sailor is honest
no depending on anyone
the ship lives unto itself
and only honest work keeps it afloat,
something workingmen on land can understand.

Whirlpool!!!
they hear it in nightmares
when the sea punishes insolence-
Suck him down!
Where are we?
Adrift, Captain. Cables cut, Engine room deserted!
Hysterical laughter snakes over the empty decks
the engines stop
the ship lolls easy port, starboard
and back, a cradle rocking
the air light, calm
strangely summer-

Six o'clock! And banging on the cabin door
There's the pilot now. And the tugs, sir.
Cast off the bow lines, Mr. Malev.
All clear!

No, the dreams mean nothing.
The earth is round, they know it.
The sea birds flying hundred of miles
over the wake of the ship,
the steel walls always humming
the lead paint, the cigarettes, liquor
the bitterness, the friendships, the ports-
It's just a restless disease seamen have
they may call it a love of freedom,
a love for the morning star
and a blue dawn at sea-
They know the earth is round,
only some make wider circles
than others.

A Sailor's Romance

A tumbler
saddled to the night serpent's back
contempt convulsing,
spitting out the dice

sky of smoke mountain clouds
and partner wind, the deadly innocents
horned moon, unmerciful judge
rupturing black sea, the executioner-

the crime?
daring, insolence-
too near the deep, fate
too near the deep.

Riverdale

Black cannon stand guard
over the jungled banks
of suspicion-

heavy boots of air,
the slow Hudson
and these staid grounds
formidable estates
of the rich

a pond
a willow tree
with drooping limbs,
it is peaceful here
among the quiet green lanes,
behind the cannon.

You are incredulous
that this could be happening
to you-

at the moment of death
suddenly
you are so alive

wait!

but then
the tumult of silence.

Chuang Tzu

You witness him
at the needle point of noon,
the agitation
the grubbing
and wrenching
rooting for the gift-

I am sitting
in the shade,
how cool it is.

For The Juggler

In a white flourecent room
with no door or windows
dark fingers arrange
and rearrange
the white furniture of intrigue,
seeking the contours of night
or some architect of order--

later, the room is silent
as if on a late afternoon in autumn,
a car passes in the street below
somewhere a radio plays
feet pad down the hall and back,
centuries pass and perhaps I am asleep
or staring at the ceiling--

there is no conclusion, Juggler
only a transparent moment
only your perfect movements.

The Door Mime

In a white space
two figures devise a door
and place it between themselves,
knocking on both sides
they seek and refuse entry
they decide upon in and out
their pockets are heavy with keys
none of which lock nor unlock the door
the figures change roles
and return unchanged,
knocking again
they devise leaving.

The Painters' Mime

The painters enter
with ladders, paint and brushes
to kill death

they are clumsy,
the audience laughs

the painters fall off their ladders
and open a door,
the devil is jubilant

a goat is sacrificed
and hangs between the ladders

the painters mock ascent
and descent

a balloon cries,
the painters exit.

In the Forest

The full pate of a moon stares-
sleep diminished, I rise
a jagged flock of clouds
wash out the light.

The downpour has ended
the forest floor is a dark sponge
I make for the stream nearby
the waters bloated and fast, draining the rain
I drink from cupped hand the icy black dye-
Tonight the betrayed are to gather here.

The barks of trees contort their faces,
their arms are listless
the wind sleeps
only the moisture lives-
I wait quietly with eyes shut
listening to the hollow drum within
some time passes
but no one arrives
there are slight eddies of movement
but nothing to be seen
more time claws by
and still they do not emerge
from the dark chambers of the forest-

Suddenly the first bird wakens
a blue haze creeps about the trees
another bird responds
my face burns
my hand discovers scratches and bruises-

They had come
but what sentence pronounced
I still do not know.

As Opposites Meet

One dances supple
a tautness within

curled fast
the plexus up
thrust man, thrust!

only lightly please
as opposites meet
too weighty, we sink

to worse hell?
one aged contends,
strike beyond death
to reach any end-

thus murderers and saints
go hand in hand.

Who Works the Rubber Bridge?

Who works the rubber bridge
when all the steel men go home?
inquired Grandpa-

We do!
chirped paper flowers, adding
and water the red bricks too!

That pleased grandpa,
pleased him to a sneeze
and assured him
that all would not decease.

Admiral Byrd

Admiral Byrd sailed by today
(I'll spit in your eye too!)
helmet, raincoat to the ankles, cold
prowling the gutterside
muttering his complaint
to the penquins at his knees-

he'd been to the poles alright
but no one recognized him-
Admiral Byrd
and no one could tell.

Christians and lions
in the coliseum
and now
the same sporting crowd
crucifies
a football.

Sly remarks

and friendships become
like a bowling alley.

In the rain soaked air
outside the Missing Persons Bureau
a piano shaped woman is waiting

an old dog sitting on hind legs
looking like a monkey
is sniffing at the fingernail moon

driving, staring up the steel ass
of the car in front of me--
is it the Vice Squad?

another Mickey Spillane night
on these long whoring streets,
another of those long, stupid nights.

A long thin black man
astride a skeleton bicycle
lollipop flowers on the terrace
thoughts of hospitals and death-

in a fish market window
a mottled brown lobster
numbly contemplates
his plateau of ice.

A bladder moon
and tigers claw
in darkness
at the ship's hull-

a Christmas
for fools
and desperados.

Water Fugue

First,
a fingernail moon—

then,
like a blue pear
two women stand
conversing in the street,
one slowly spinning
an open umbrella
on the nape of shoulder,
so flirtatious—

and now,
a puffed up parakeet
looking like a green buffalo,
standing on one claw
conversing by the window
with the rain.

Stars whisper
in echoes
across the Universe-
I do not strain
my eyes.

In the Weeds

Late night rearranging scenes
from pieces of a broken egg shell

darts slung inaccurately
bounce off their targets
and further crack
the circle of unsettled minds,
sentences trail off dimly
into the blue morning
and a mist surrounds companions
scattered incoherently

in the weeds.

In the Weeds

Late night rearranging scenes
from pieces of a broken egg shell

darts slung inaccurately
bounce off their targets
and further crack
the circle of unsettled minds,
sentences trail off dimly
into the blue morning
and a mist surrounds companions
scattered incoherently

in the weeds.

This Year

This year
solace comes
like Christmas
too early
and prepackaged

or
like an old friend
lost to Jesus

(please
come and save him
quick).

Lost
as the page turned
I lost it
in a pit
of quick
reflection
past, when
back then
an old hen
in her pen
took on ten.....

whoops

in Gobi
a ship
slips by.

In a Bank

In a bank
one must not loiter
in a bank
one must come and go
a bank lives on tip toe
a bank is not a joke.

The Scarlet-Capped Black Boy

Any flourescence
                in a subway car
is muffled
          by the blue soot
and dull air
            of overcoats
and woolen faces
              until
a scarlet-capped
            black boy
rolls back the door
              at one end
of the pitching,
          rolling car
and swinging
        jauntily
round poles
        over shoes
through eyeglasses,
              newspapers
and purses,
        disrupts

the hypnotic dirge
            with red life.

a
fau
cet
drip
ping
will
set
you
mad
then
quick
don't
think
take
aim
hell
blast
it
off
!

Wind
washes trees
and loosens
their joy-

I, too
am bound
by this same chance breeze.

A stadium world
bellowing
deaf-

cup in hand
cane and rattle
he counts the days
penny
by penny.

on seeing a dishevelled man
stamp out the door
of some cheap hotel
while fire engines are parked outside
in the streets
lights flashing,
sirens, etc.

I May Not Be Frank Sinatra

I may not be Frank Sinatra
but when I'm sleeping in my room
at two in the afternoon
after a long night out,
I don't want to be woken up
by some fireman
trouncing up and down the hall
axing down my door
and screaming at me to get out
cause the building's on fire-
At least he could give me time
to get a goddamn cigarette lit.

One Claim

To surrender
everything

only a handful
withheld

but even one claim
stops up
the pocket of tears-

then,
how to plead?

You Know This Place

You know this place,
there is nothing easier-

From the ceiling the music descends
calming, just audible before a thought
the lights, the counter
all bright and clean
the stools of orange cushion
the walls placidly blue
the stainless steel cow in action
dispensing milk from a white plastic udder-
here and there a soft shoed nurse
smiles behind a black apron
and skims across the linoleum
with coffee and the weather for some cowboys-
the hamburger heat
the dishes clashing
the cash register ringing
plate glass windows onto the parking lot-

with eyes closed
I never feel safer,
nothing is easier.

A Bust of Shakespeare Found in the Sand

Shakespeare, beached
his plastic nose flattened,
the crevices of his face filled
with gray sand-

Huntington Beach, L.A.
and behind us the oil
is being sucked up
by giant steel locusts-
I feel a great sympathy
for those enslaved insects
because they have a cruel Queen
who will never release them

and because
because of those blondes
with their tan, smooth bodies
and white bikinis
who look so great from a distance-
I stroll down the beach
and try to talk to a few of them
then I stroll back up the beach
gazing into the glimmering ocean-

perhaps the locusts alwasy have their work
but I'm left feeling like Shakespeare
beached, with his plastic nose
flattened into the sand.

Returning from a Job Interview

A soiled and yellow collar
on the shirt of the city

trees turn gray
along the traffic route of ants

the heat irons everything flat,
masks melt

every position seems uncomfortable
but at last something,

the car radiator,
threatens life.

The flourescent airport
at 3:30 AM
is not the place
to leer
at a petite pubescent
in tight blue jeans
and long blond hair-

she might think
you're wierd
or something,
gee.

Cat

In a square
of fur sunlight

the afternoon
stretches

but
cannot keep

his eyes

open.

A Summer Morning

Purple testes
weigh down
the branched member
of a plum tree.

On the Runway

Charging bulls
wild horses
singing lariats
painted
from dawn blue clouds
over the broad
Texas horizon.

Scratches

scrawls of light
against blackened earth

gentle tilt
of giant metal wing

face
in a round hole

horizon
of torn flames.

From a Window Seat, Miles High

Spine of rock
washed blacks, bled red
rusted greens of rock
buttress, rift
moldings of rock
plateau of rock
fingers, hands
veins clawed, scraped
rolled over
pounded, torn
"unshaped by thought"
still, luminescent still
not even a shrub comes near
no plan
but the plans of rock.

Landing Approach

It's only a fog we are passing through
a material like flannel
while the sky drifts upward
out of reach
and the blue lit circuitry of the runway
isolates safety.

In a Waiting Room

A woman reading a purple newspaper wherein the Queen of Sudan having stooped to give a small orange to a beggar has accidently cut his thumb withherlong black fingernails and drawn blood whereuponshetakes the thumb in her mouthandsucks the wound while the beggar swoons and the woman reading thepurple newspaperiscalled, Next!

Helping the Artist to Hang Paintings

Therefore, their world
being upside down
comes the expression
"having to stand
on one's head"
and the back,
being more favorable
than the front,
an angle occurs
at the juncture
of head and neck
whereupon
one nears the place
of feeling
"light-headed"
so that finally
"to lose one's head,"
expresses
the most subtle
and complete
point of
comprehension.

Madame de Pompadour at the Legion of Honor

They cheated me.
She said it like that,
simply
and she wasn't angry
only a little tired,
would we mind if she lay down a bit?

From a gallery of pink-skinned cupids
her eyes transfix
to blue bubble heaven.
The ceiling dislodges itself
and crashes down
quietly
in her face.

At the Museum

Unlike those waiting,
neither called for
nor remembered,
I shall retire
one day
into a Chinese
landscape painting.

Leaves

Tatters of autumn
wild
with wind grinding through-

torn sails
on the mainmast
of a great ghost ship.

Water Scenario

I.

Two persons discover themselves
in a vast dark water.
With all hands and feet
they swim for a distant light

II.

Two persons discover themselves
in a vast dark water.
They spot a faint light
in the distance.
One cares to swim for that light,
the other does not.

III.

Two persons discover themselves
in a vast dark water.
Instantly a motorboat rescues them.

Then let a man be without tears!
Let him be dry and hard
with no mooring
but for birth and death,
cursing that which plows wide chasms
in faith and effort
and makes love
an ever impassable hedge of thorns
waving always banners of roses.
Let him hit and break glass
and let him flee
as he says,
to live upon the backs of winds
and shout into the throat of the sky.
Out of the way,
let him go!

The Poet in Love

Milk sop love
nougat with nuts
chocolate squares
of Valentine's heart

dump them all
in rivers of tar
and give me Violence!
,
love's only blood.

In Coupled Night

The pain
that dreads
relief.

The Kiss

He stuffed her mouth
with a kiss

No! Wait!
she cried

too late-
the glue of love.

No, she says, she doesn't want
to cry on me and that finger place
between her breasts, that too
is a deep cry but the afternoon
weaving like jazz through smoke
mixes many streams, many waters
salty and sweet and we, on our
raft of love, somewhere between
where we were and where we should be,
that current outside of things
crying, laughing, crazy, happy
(I really haven't been there for
a long time) means for a few hours,
oh, not very poetically put,
everything.

The Scent of Rain

Time
and the rain
fall

while they slept
we wandered in the night
their windows were sealed
and from their beds no light issued
the streets were silent,
the resolution of silence
which neither condemns nor absolves
and we were diseased with life
beyond the last of the revellers
while they fled like fugitives
into sleep
we stood

and time fell
and we could not stop its fall
but for the scent
of the rain.

A Farewell

The jaundice lit bus depot
evening loitering outside,
when you buy a ticket
the ground sticks to your foot-

later, on the bridge
a drunk flags down the car
he needs a match
climbs in
says he's been happy for 15 days
or is it 25? anyway,
light? oh yeah, thanks

turn my eyes inward darling
from the dizzy circling outside
yes, let's run off
you and I
stepping over the corpses, come-

black penned lines swirl around the pasty eyes
of the pillow of a counter girl dispensing hamburgers
a cloudburst of beard bobs by the window
Gate 32!
write, call, come up!
think of me-

my last dollar for his next drink
right here
dump him in the lap of the city-
the night is drowning
and no one can swim.

The Dilemma of C.

She said: I never felt so alone
as when he made love to me.
It made me realize how,
in the end,
we are always left alone.

Then the car slid out of control
and we crashed down an icy cliff.
When I came to,
everything was crystal and still.
I screamed for him,
he answerd.
We were both alive, unhurt.
The roof, the glass
the whole thing was smashed in.
We were upside down
but alive.

We walked back to the lodge in silence
and entered like ghosts.
No one knew if we had ever left
or returned
or what had happened in between.
We were ghosts,
the car lying at the bottom of that ledge,
perhaps our bodies still inside.

Somehow we had transcended death
but now even that is lost.
At midnight he wakens
and covers me with hardness.
I rouse myself
but we'll never go there again.

After the Film

I don't think you've ever been alone
and you don't know what love is either—

a trolley with bells and rumbling
a crowd on the piazza
a gray Italian film bustles and crackles by
on the TV,
I shut the lights off early
recall your words

and mumble good night
to limbs hanging in the closet,
a profusion of sifting faces
I am trying to get through the crowd
the trolley begins to pull away
you are waving a handkerchief—

good-bye, good-bye!

In the blue light
of love
I am possessed
unafraid

the bizarre black caress
of nylon and leather
the fever of command and consent

a full moon glares
through an iron gate
a strange land
forbidden yet blessed.

In blue smoke German she sings:

You don't know how good I am for you
Come here, sit down beside me
Don't hurt me now
I won't be sad, darling

The night has no beams to hold on to
My kisses are not like lollipops
It's late, don't go
Wait 'til the morning

Don't like long good byes either
No talk, it'll be easier
I'll leave your picture on the wall
But when you get back, I'll be gone

You don't know how good I am for you
Come here, sit down beside me
Don't hurt me now
I won't be sad, darling.

Moon Goddess

Above a pale batik of clouds
the Moon Goddess
with ivory brown eyes
slowly rubs against the African night

She is raising herself up
into the lap of dreams
giving her hips
to the wide river
opening her lips
to the glistening water buffalo

That coquette makes the Earth
sullen with envy
A winter knife will slash that whore
then Moon Goddess will try forever
to be whole again

But for now
she licks the thighs of the great banyan tree
and laughing softly
she tilts her domed brow
and beckons to the Sun.

OK, had to let you see this, Los Angeles, 1985. My big move from SF on my career path to becoming the next Tom Cruise, moving to Hollywood in 1980. This was at the Gardner Stage in Hollywood in *The Connection* by Jack Gelber written in 1959 and first produced in NYC by The Living Theatre. It is a gritty ensemble piece about a depressing group of junkies waiting for their connection to show up. Boritzer won the 1985 Best Actor Award by Drama-Logue Magazine, the now defunct weekly West Coast theater trade publication, for the role of Leach, whose apartment the junkies use while waiting for Cowboy (the connection) to show up.

"Holiday Greetings from all of us!" - Etan Boritzer

Uh, my own creative publicity card during my early Hollywood years. I was acting and writing until 1989, actually moving up in town until the Writers Guild strike hit and there was no work for anyone for a year. That's when I quit show biz and started our contemporary fine art gallery in Santa Monica.

Patricia Eltinge

Patricia Eltinge, the Love of My Life! Patricia Eltinge, dream analyst/book author and relationship expert. I asked God to please let me get this *man/woman thing* right just once in my life, and thankfully we met in 2017 through a mutual friend when Patricia was looking for a publisher for her book *The Dream Class*. We began working on the book, then had dinners together and then walks on the beach. It was a true literary romance! And it turned out that all the time I was looking for true love, Patricia lived only 2 blocks away. Patricia is a living poem of beauty, wisdom, wit and (*ha*) endurance!

ThankyaLordy! ThankyaLordy!
Thank you, my Goddess, my *shakti*, my *devi*, my *dakini*, my *tantrika!*
Please don't ever kick me out, honey. I promise I'll be good!

www.ingramcontent.com/pod-product-compliance
Lightning Source LLC
LaVergne TN
LVHW061046070526
838201LV00074B/5191